Aspects of the Liturgical Year in Cappadocia (325–430)

PATRISTIC STUDIES

Gerald Bray
General Editor

Vol. 7

PETER LANG
New York • Washington, D.C./Baltimore • Bern
Frankfurt am Main • Berlin • Brussels • Vienna • Oxford

Jill Burnett Comings

ASPECTS OF THE LITURGICAL YEAR IN CAPPADOCIA (325–430)

PETER LANG
New York • Washington, D.C./Baltimore • Bern
Frankfurt am Main • Berlin • Brussels • Vienna • Oxford

BV
30
.C597
2005

Library of Congress Cataloging-in-Publication Data

Comings, Jill Burnett.
Aspects of the liturgical year in Cappadocia (325–430) / Jill Burnett Comings.
p. cm. — (Patristic studies ; v. 7)
Includes bibliographical references and index.
1. Church year—Turkey—Cappadocia. 2. Cappadocia (Turkey)—Church history.
I. Title. II. Series: Patristic studies (Peter Lang Publishing); v. 7.
BV30.C597   263'.9'093934—dc22   2004021352
ISBN 0-8204-7464-9
ISSN 1094-6217

Bibliographic information published by **Die Deutsche Bibliothek.**
Die Deutsche Bibliothek lists this publication in the "Deutsche
Nationalbibliografie"; detailed bibliographic data is available
on the Internet at http://dnb.ddb.de/.

The paper in this book meets the guidelines for permanence and durability
of the Committee on Production Guidelines for Book Longevity
of the Council of Library Resources.

© 2005 Peter Lang Publishing, Inc., New York
275 Seventh Avenue, 28th Floor, New York, NY 10001
www.peterlangusa.com

All rights reserved.
Reprint or reproduction, even partially, in all forms such as microfilm,
xerography, microfiche, microcard, and offset strictly prohibited.

Printed in Germany

Table of Contents

Acknowledgments

This book and the dissertation upon which it is based would not have come to be were it not for the support, assistance and enthusiasm of many people—teachers, colleagues, family and friends.

Special gratitude to the Right Reverend Dr. J. Neil Alexander, mentor and friend, for directing the dissertation, but even more for introducing me to the world of liturgical studies in a seminary course almost 15 years ago—and for his friendship and crucial role in my scholarly formation. Many thanks also to the Reverend Dr. John F. Baldovin, S.J. and the Reverend Dr. Robin A. Leaver for serving on my dissertation committee, offering expertise and encouragement, as well as valued suggestions for strengthening my work. Despite their great assistance, the responsibility for the contents of the book and any inadequacies therein remain mine alone.

I am also indebted to the Reverend Dr. Thomas J. Talley for his gracious help in understanding ancient calendars and to my research assistant, Mr. J. Brent Bates, who spent many hours formatting, proofreading, helping to transform dissertation into book. I would also like to thank the folks at Peter Lang Publishing, for their assistance and much-appreciated patience as I figured out the book-publishing process and Dr. Gerald Bray, Series Editor, for reading the manuscript and improving the work with his helpful input.

On a more personal note, I want to thank those who in so many ways have loved and supported me through this process, especially Mom and Dad, Barbara and Leslie, and the interdisciplinary study group at Drew.

Finally and most especially, to my husband, Ben, *sine quo non*, master of the mysteries of my word processing program, I owe a huge debt of gratitude, not only for his many, many hours of technical help, but also for his enthusiasm for my work and unwavering love.

Abbreviations

ANF	*Ante-Nicene Fathers*
ESGN	*The Easter Sermons of Gregory of Nyssa*
FOTC	*The Fathers of the Church*
GNH	*Gregory of Nyssa Homepage*
GNO	*Gregorii Nysseni Opera*
HM	Hieronymian Martyrology
NPNF	*Nicene and Post-Nicene Fathers*
SM	Syriac Martyrology
Typikon	*The Typikon of the Great Church*

Psalm numbers given are those of the Septuagint, as this is the numbering system used in most of the critical editions of the Greek texts of these sermons.

Chapter 1

Introduction: Multiple Contexts

The fourth century was a time of significant change for the Christian churches of the Roman Empire, not least in matters liturgical. The toleration, legalization and establishment of Christianity under the emperors Constantine and Theodosius I are often cited as the main catalysts for much of this change; for example, the end of the threat of state-sponsored persecution contributed greatly to the change of worship venue from private (domestic) space to public space, which, along with imperial patronage of the newly licit religion, led to increased liturgical ceremonial as well as other developments. In addition, the state became involved in conciliar efforts to define "orthodox" doctrine and to condemn as "heretics" those whose beliefs differed from those norms. However, as Paul Bradshaw cautions, "[t]he so-called Constantinian revolution served as much to intensify existing trends as it did to initiate new ones."[1]

Both of these dynamics were at play in the development of the cycle of feasts, fasts and other commemorations known as the liturgical year. The central feast of the annual cycle—Pascha—had been universally celebrated in one form or another since the end of the second century, and martyrs' feasts and other observances continued to be added to the calendar. However, major changes in the structures and patterns of the liturgical year did take place in the wake of the Peace of Constantine, and, by the end of the fourth century, the calendars of the various churches shared a common basic structure that many Christians today would recognize.

The history of these fourth-century liturgical year developments has been the subject of extensive research.[2] However, a major lacuna in our knowledge of this early development concerns Cappadocia, an important province of Asia Minor in the Eastern Roman Empire. Earlier scholarship has concentrated on developments in Jerusalem and Rome, as well as somewhat later developments in the Gallican West, but while Cappadocian sources have been used to map such areas as the solidification of Nicene trinitarian doctrine and the integration of Greek philosophical models and Christianity, what these sources reveal about the development of the liturgical year in fourth-century Cappadocia remains largely uncharted territory.

This study attempts to fill in that area of the map, gathering together the Cappadocian data in order to conduct a comprehensive examination of the annual cycle of feasts and fasts as it existed and evolved in this area between the Councils of Nicea (325) and Ephesus (431). The primary textual sources for this investigation are the liturgical year homilies of four Cappadocian figures and one Pontic figure[3] who preached and wrote during the fourth century in various locations in Asia Minor—Basil of Caesarea, Gregory of Nazianzus, Gregory of Nyssa, Amphilochius of Iconium and Asterius of Amaseia—whose influence in other liturgical and doctrinal matters is well known, but whose impact on the development of the liturgical year has not been systematically or comprehensively explored. Some scholars researching the liturgical year *have* mined this body of material to isolate discrete texts for comparison with more well-known Western sources, but heretofore no attempt has been made to study these homilies as a whole and in relation to each other in order to get a picture of what the annual liturgical year cycles looked like in Cappadocia in this period.

This chapter will define the project and set it in its multiple contexts. The first section sets the parameters of the project in terms of what primary sources were selected, why they were selected, what problems of interpretation they present, according to what method they will be analyzed, and how the results are organized. The second section maps out the cultural and ecclesio-political contexts in which these developments took place in Cappadocia and environs, as well as the social or literary relationships that existed among the group of church leaders on which the project focuses. Based on these contextual beginnings, I hope to demonstrate the need for the project and how it will further the discussion about liturgical year developments in the fourth century.

Sources, Method and Organization

One advantage of focusing on homiletical texts is the opportunity they afford to get fairly close to what the faithful were being taught from pulpits about the purposes and meanings of these observances, although the length and complexity of some of these texts suggest that we are in the presence of homilies edited and expanded for publication, not intended for the parish.

One drawback is that we still only get to know what these purposes and meanings were from the *bishops'* points of view; only occasionally do we get a glimpse of other interpretations and practices, if they existed, and even then, it is usually through the lens of episcopal disapproval. However, given the lack of direct evidence from the faithful of fourth-century Cappadocia, these homilies may represent our closest link to how the feasts and fasts were actually observed, at least in a few important centers of Cappadocian Christianity.[4]

The data from these homilies[5] are supplemented by information from other homilies, treatises and letters composed by these figures. In addition, primary sources from other areas of the Roman Empire are used for comparison. Martyrological sources are also used. The "Hieronymian Martyrology,"[6] so-called because of its earlier erroneous attribution to Jerome, is a compilation of several local martyrologies. It was produced in Italy in the second half of the fifth century, and a Gallican recension, from which all extant manuscripts of the HM are derived, was made around 600. The sources used in this compilation include a local martyrology from Rome and general martyrologies from Italy, Africa and the East.[7] This Eastern martyrology is what interests us most. In 1866 *The Journal of Sacred Literature* published the Syriac Martyrology[8] discovered by W. Wright,[9] and Victor De Buck subsequently demonstrated its relationship to the HM.[10] Hippolyte Delehaye notes that the establishment of this relationship helped scholars to recognize "the existence of a general martyrology of the Orient, written in Greek at Nicomedia, and which served as a source for the 'Hieronymian'."[11] Elsewhere, Delehaye writes that the SM is a summary of this earlier Greek martyrology, which dates from before 411.[12] Because the original Greek source is roughly contemporary with the works of our preachers, especially those of Asterius, the information contained in the Syriac summary, as reconstructed by DeRossi and Duchesne, is used to supplement the Cappadocian sources where possible, particularly in Chapter 4. Occasionally, the later recensions of the HM are also cited, not as an indication of fourth-century Cappadocian practice but as interesting information about what became the practice in these areas somewhat later. The *Typikon of the Great Church*,[13] the earliest manuscript of which dates from the late ninth or early tenth century[14] and reflects practices in Constantinople, is also cited for the information it gives about later practice. The HM and *Typikon* provide points of temporal comparison to supplement our concern to include points of geographical comparison.

The methodological principles of Robert Taft, the current leading theoretician and practitioner of the Anton Baumstark school of comparative liturgiology,[15] underlie the research and writing of this book. The aim of this method, which Taft calls "the comparative historico-textual and structural study of liturgy,"[16] is to "reconstitute the past from its leftover débris" by "sifting and analyzing, classifying and comparing, liturgical texts and units within and across traditions."[17] The goal is to gather data and then, through structural analysis and comparison, to create an interpretive framework that leads to understanding and historical reconstruction. The data are not new; Greek texts of all of these homilies exist in various critical editions, and translations are available, particularly in French and German, for many of them, and so this material is accessible to scholars. Using the "comparative historico-textual and structural" method to study the liturgical homilies of the Cappadocians will enable us to see the relationship between these texts and at least a hypothetical outline of the liturgical year in fourth-century Cappadocia, as well as to understand what was changing and what factors contributed to these changes.

One of Taft's most important correctives to Baumstark's comparative method is that, while Baumstark focused on the comparison of *similarities* among practices across regions, time periods and traditions, Taft is just as interested in comparing the *differences*.[18] In addition, while Taft begins with structural analysis of liturgical units, he insists that "this analysis is not carried on in a vacuum. There must be a constant dialectic between structural analysis and historical research."[19] With these two correctives as guides, the interpretive work of this study is built upon the recognition that, while fourth-century Cappadocia's liturgical calendar was undoubtedly being shaped by some of the same forces that were influencing the calendars of other regions, the particularities of time and place, as well as cultural and ecclesio-political contexts, rendered its development unique in many ways. The liturgical year data from fourth-century and early fifth-century Cappadocia are gathered together for, I believe, the first time in English and allowed to speak for themselves. Data from other regions is interspersed but not in order to fill in the gaps; for the most part they are used to show what could also have happened in Cappadocia but did not, highlighting the localized nature of these calendrical developments. The historical research component of the study's dialectic will focus on Cappadocia's ecclesio-political situation during this period, especially on the doctrinal controversies in which each of these five figures was involved to some degree.

In his eulogy for his brother Basil, Gregory of Nyssa told his congregation, "God has set up the praiseworthy order to these annual feasts of ours, which, by means of a certain fixed sequence, we have both already celebrated and we celebrate again."[20] It is important to note that our preachers *did* perceive their collection of fasts and feasts as an annual cycle, observed according to a "certain fixed sequence," but there is no evidence in their works of a distinction among Paschal, Nativity and Sanctoral sub-cycles. This distinction is made here for organizational purposes only. Hence, after this introductory chapter establishing the project's purpose, parameters and contexts, the primary evidence is presented in three chapters. Chapter 2 addresses Pascha and its related feasts and fasts. Chapter 3 discusses Epiphany, Christmas and their constellation of observances. Chapter 4 considers feasts celebrating the lives and deaths of saints and martyrs. Chapter 5 draws our findings together in a concluding synthesis suggesting that the liturgical year was, among other things, a complex means of communication used by our preachers to teach what was, in their opinion, right belief, to refute the ideas of those who disagreed, and to establish and solidify relationships.

Contexts and Relationships

The kingdom of Cappadocia was a Roman dependency since 191 B.C. and was fully annexed by Rome in 17 A.D.[21] In the year 72, Vespasian replaced the procurator of Cappadocia with a consular legate, who was also responsible for Galatia, Paphlagonia, Pontus Galacticus, Pontus Polemoniacus and Armenia Minor. Trajan, who ruled from 107 to 113, divided this huge area into two separate provinces. Armenia Minor and Pontus were left under the rule of the consular legate of Cappadocia, until in his massive administrative restructuring of the empire, Diocletian divided Cappadocia. In 371 or 372, the Arian Emperor Valens further divided the western region into Cappadocia Prima, whose capital remained Caesarea, and Cappadocia Secunda, whose capital was established at Tyana. This last administrative move proved vexing for Basil; because ecclesiastical organization was based on civil organization, Basil stood to lose much of his jurisdiction to Anthimus of Tyana.[22] We will have occasion to explore this tension further in later chapters.

We do not know for sure when Christianity came to Cappadocia. In a letter encouraging the presbyters of Nicomedia to select a new bishop wisely, Gregory of Nyssa reminds them that suitability to such a post is not determined by wealth, education or social status but by spiritual status. He gives several examples of churches that chose humble, uneducated men over wealthy officials or those trained in philosophy and rhetoric. Crete selected Titus, Jerusalem chose James, and Cappadocia preferred the centurion who, according to Matthew 27.54 and its parallels, confessed Christ's divinity at the moment of Christ's death.[23] Whether or not this centurion was an early Cappadocian bishop, Christianity may actually have come to the region by way of the Jewish community there. Apparently, there were Jews in Cappadocia in the first century A.D., since residents of Cappadocia were among the Jews and converts to Judaism who had traveled to Jerusalem for Pentecost, according to Acts 2.9.

By around 100 there were also Christians in the region; the elect in Cappadocia are among those to whom 1 Peter is addressed.[24] Eusebius of Caesarea in Palestine mentions a tradition that Peter was the apostle assigned to preach to the Jews of the Dispersion who were living in Pontus, Galatia, Bithynia, Cappadocia and Asia.[25] Eusebius also refers to epistles written to various churches by Dionysius, bishop of Corinth around 170.[26] One of these letters was written to the church of Amastris in Pontus and refers specifically to its bishop, Palmas, who, as Eusebius later tells us, presided at a synod to address the issue of the date of Easter.[27] At the turn of the second to the third century, Tertullian mentions that Cappadocian Christians were suffering persecution at the hands of one Claudius Lucius Herminianus, who was angry with his wife for converting to Christianity and took his wrath out on the Christians of the area.[28] According to Eusebius, Alexander, who later became bishop of Jerusalem and ordained Origen,[29] was a bishop in Cappadocia around this same time, although we do not know which city was his see.[30] Somewhat later in the third century, Christianity in Cappadocia apparently benefited greatly from the missionary efforts of Gregory Thaumaturgus, who was born in Cappadocian Pontus between 210 and 215, was a student of Origen in Caesarea of Palestine from about 233 to 238, and was conscripted by the metropolitan bishop of Amaseia, Phaidimos, to be bishop of Neocaesarea. He led the Neocaesarean community through the Decian persecution of 250–251 and the Gothic invasions of Pontus several years later. According to Eusebius, he attended the synod at Antioch in 264 at which Paul of Samosata was condemned.[31] He probably died during the reign of Aurelian (270–275).[32] Basil credits Gregory Thaumaturgus with converting Pontus; in *De Spiritu Sancto*, he writes:

> But where shall I rank the great Gregory, and the words uttered by him? Shall we not place among Apostles and Prophets a man who walked by the same Spirit as they (2 Cor. xii.18); who never through all his days diverged from the footprints of the saints; who maintained, as long as he lived, the exact principles of evangelical citizenship? I am sure that we shall do the truth a wrong if we refuse to number that soul with the people of God, shining as it did like a beacon in the Church of God; for by the fellow-working of the Spirit the power which he had over demons was tremendous, and so gifted was he with the grace of the word "for obedience to the faith among...the nations" (Rom. i.5), that, although only seventeen Christians were handed over to him, he brought the whole people alike in town and country through knowledge to God.[33]

Gregory of Nyssa describes how Gregory quickly built a congregation from these seventeen Christians whom he had inherited upon consecration.[34] Macrina the Elder, paternal grandmother of Basil and Gregory, was acquainted with some of his disciples.[35]

We also know of a Firmilian, who was bishop of Caesarea in Cappadocia around the time Gregory Thaumaturgus was having such a successful episcopate in Neocaesarea. Firmilian corresponded with Cyprian of Carthage over the issue of rebaptizing those who had been baptized by heretics.[36]

We know very little about these early Cappadocian bishops, and, unfortunately, little remains of any of their writings. There are several extant works composed by Gregory Thaumaturgus, but the one liturgical year homily attributed to him has been shown to be spurious.[37] An abundance of primary sources from this area exists only from after the Council of Nicea, particularly from the pens of the five preachers on whom this project focuses. It is primarily because of this abundance of information that these five men were chosen; however, the relationships that existed among them are another factor. We have mentioned the highly localized nature of calendrical developments in the churches of the Roman Empire. Did the unique situation in Cappadocia, where Basil had so much influence over who occupied what see and saw to it that his friends and relatives occupied the ones that most secured his own position, result in more sharing among the various churches when it came to liturgical year observances? This is a question that will be addressed at various points in the chapters that follow. Here our concern is to establish the relationships.[38] Basil and Gregory of Nyssa were brothers, born

c. 330 and c. 335, respectively, into a fairly affluent and prominent Christian family, who owned property in both Cappadocia and Pontus.[39] Basil was educated in Caesarea, Constantinople and Athens, where he met and be-friended Gregory of Nazianzus.[40] Little is known about Gregory of Nyssa's education, although in a letter to Libanius, Basil's teacher in Constantinople, Gregory himself credits Basil with being his teacher.[41] Their relationship was complex and, at times, strained. Basil's consecration as Bishop of Caesarea in 370 was opposed by many,[42] including his own uncle, Gregory, who was a bishop of some unspecified Cappadocian see. Brother Gregory tried to effect a reconciliation between the two by forging—or having someone else forge—three letters from Uncle Gregory to Basil.[43] When the elder Gregory denied having written the letters, Basil wrote to his brother, chastising him for being so naïve but also wishing for some commiseration from him. He writes:

> I have written this to upbraid you for your simplicity—which I consider not only unbecoming in a Christian, but especially inappropriate at the present time—in or-der that for the future you may both watch over youself [sic] and spare me, since—for I must speak to you frankly—you are untrustworthy as a messenger in such mat-ters. Yet, whoever they may be who wrote, we have answered them as was proper. Therefore, whether you yourself were laying this trap for me or had really received from the bishops the letter which you sent me, you have my answer. In fact, since you are our brother still mindful of the ties of nature, and do not look upon us as an enemy, you should have been otherwise concerned at the present, seeing that we have entered upon a life which, because it exceeds our strength, wears away our body and even afflicts our soul. Still, since you have in this way become involved in the warfare, you ought, therefore, to be at hand now and to share the troubles.[44]

Basil also wrote directly to his uncle, requesting a meeting to resolve their differences,[45] but we do not know if such a meeting or resolution ever occurred. We do know that further tensions continued to strain the relation-ship between Basil and his brother Gregory. Following Valens's partition of Cappadocia in 371/372, Basil, apparently trying to strengthen his suddenly weakened position, began placing loyal family members and friends in the sees of Anthimus's Cappadocia Secunda.[46] Among these were his dear friend Gregory of Nazianzus (c. 330–c. 390) and his brother Gregory, whom in 372 Basil consecrated to the sees of Sasima (created by Basil) and Nyssa, respec-tively. The latter Gregory, however, continued to make Basil uneasy; in 372 or 373 Basil wrote to Eusebius of Samosata to invite him to a synod and to request his assistance with a number of matters, including Gregory of

Nyssa's synod-organizing activities in Ancyra, which Basil interpreted as a scheme against him.[47]

Gregory of Nazianzus reluctantly accepted the see of Sasima but in all likelihood was never able to do the job because of resistance from Anthimus. By autumn, Gregory was back in Nazianzus, assisting his father, who was the bishop there. His formerly very close friendship with Basil never recovered from the injury of having been thus used. Gregory complained often about Basil's "tyranny" in forcing him to forfeit his life of contemplation in favor of an ecclesiastical career,[48] even during the last decade of his life. In his poem, *Concerning His Own Life*, written early in 382,[49] Gregory reflects bitterly on the incident:

> Midway along the high road through Cappadocia, where the road divides into three, there's a stopping place. It's without water or vegetation, not quite civilized, a thoroughly deplorable and cramped little village. There's dust all around the place, the din of wagons, laments, groans, tax officials, implements of torture, and public stocks. The population consists of casuals and vagrants. Such was my church of Sasima. He who was surrounded by fifty *chorepiscopi* was so magnanimous as to make me incumbent here. The whole idea was to get the better of a violent intruder by founding a new see. And among his warrior friends apparently I held first place. O yes, I was an able fighter once, wounds that are blessed being no great disaster. For, added to the features I've already enumerated, that particular see couldn't be held without bloodshed. It was a no man's land between two rival bishops. A division of our native province, which set up two metropolises for the small towns, gave occasion for the outbreak of a fearful brawl. The pretext was souls; but in fact, of course, it was a desire for control, control (I hesitate to say it) of taxes and contributions, which have the whole world in a miserable commotion.[50]

At this point of Gregory's life, ten years after the incident and three years after Basil's death in 379, his feelings were ambivalent, as he himself remarks. He had praised Basil at great length in a funeral oration, yet he could not forget what had happened between them. He writes:

> Once I got a taste of trouble, disaster followed disaster. Basil, the closest of our friends, came to visit us. (I should like to pass over intervening events in silence, lest I seem to speak in insulting terms about a man whose eulogy I've just pronounced.) He came, alas for the story, but I must tell it all the same. He was to prove another father to me, and a far more burdensome one. My real father, even though he tyrannized over me, I must shelter; but no such duty holds in his case, where friendship actually brought injury instead of deliverance from trouble. I cannot know whether I should lay more blame on my own sins, which often indeed have tortured me (the incident is always fresh and rankling in my mind), or on the high-handed style you acquired with the throne, O best of men.[51]

One of the results of this estrangement between Basil and his friend Gregory was that Basil had to cultivate other friendships in order to garner support. An important example of this was his friendship with Amphilochius, Cappadocian rhetor and lawyer,[52] cousin of Gregory of Nazianzus on his mother's side and future bishop of Iconium. Amphilochius (c. 340–395) received at least part of his education with Libanius in Constantinople. Around 362, he decided to renounce his public life in favor of ascetic retirement at Ozizala, near Nazianzus. In 373, Basil wrote to him, under the name of Amphilochius's friend Heracleidas, who was living at Basil's hospital in Caesarea.[53] In Heracleidas's name, Basil tried to lure Amphilochius away from his eremitic asceticism into an asceticism of service to others at Basil's hospital.[54] Instead, Amphilochius was consecrated bishop of Iconium in that same year.[55] We do not know for sure whether Basil had anything to do with the choice of Amphilochius for the see of Iconium, but in a letter to Eusebius of Samosata, Basil says that the church there, which had just lost its bishop, Faustinus, had invited him to visit and to "give it a bishop." He desired advice from Eusebius as to whether he "should not refuse to perform ordinations beyond our boundaries," but it is likely that he had at least some influence in the matter.[56]

After Amphilochius's consecration, he and Basil embarked upon a very friendly and close mentor/protégé relationship. Amphilochius often asked for advice and information; Basil responded copiously, sometimes with brief but affectionate greetings,[57] sometimes with more substantial collections of Basil's thoughts on a wide range of topics from ecclesiastical polity to church discipline to controverted theological points. The so-called "canonical letters"[58] are the most well-known of this latter group. Philip Rousseau points out that in these letters, Basil takes the situation in Iconium into account when advising Amphilochius. Rousseau writes, "Just as, in the *Asceticon*, Basil created ad hoc 'rules' for ascetic disciples, so, in these letters, he gave advice on the church order to be followed in Iconium. While he appealed characteristically to the broader traditions of the Church, he applied his principles in a precise way to the needs of the church under Amphilochius's care...."[59] Through these letters Basil exerted a great deal of influence over the church in Iconium, if, as seems likely, Amphilochius followed Basil's advice. Unfortunately, the letters contain more information about theological issues than about liturgical year questions, but they, along with other letters and Basil's treatise *De Spiritu Sancto*, which he dedicated to Amphilochius, do contain some clues.

Basil's cultivation of friendship with and mentorship of Amphilochius took place after Basil's estrangement from Gregory of Nazianzus. Gregory considered Amphilochius's consecration to be another example of Basil's "tyranny."[60]

The relationships did not all involve Basil. Gregory of Nazianzus and Gregory of Nyssa corresponded with each other. When the latter Gregory gave up his vocation as a reader in the church and became a professor of rhetoric, the former Gregory wrote to chastise him and to encourage him to return to church work.[61] During his banishment by Valens for refusing to attend a synod convened to look into some charges brought against him by Demosthenes, the Vicar of the civil diocese of Pontus, Gregory of Nyssa apparently wrote letters, no longer extant, to Gregory of Nazianzus. Gregory of Nazianzus's replies do survive.[62] Nazianzus also wrote to Nyssa on several other occasions, including the death of Basil, the resignation by Gregory of Nazianzus of the see of Constantinople, and the death of Gregory of Nyssa's wife, Theosebia.[63]

Gregory of Nazianzus and Amphilochius corresponded with each other, both before and after the latter embarked upon his ecclesiastical career. Gregory wrote several letters to his younger cousin, concerning everything from Amphilochius's early legal troubles in Constantinople to matters of ecclesiastical politics to requests for some of the vegetables he was growing in his solitude at Ozizala.[64] The correspondence was not one-sided; in one letter, Gregory refers gratefully to the many letters he has received from Amphilochius.[65]

Gregory of Nyssa wrote to Amphilochius, requesting that the latter send masons and other workers to help with the construction of the Church of the Martyrs. Apparently, there had already been some correspondence about this matter, since Gregory refers to reluctance on the part of Amphilochius to get involved in the project and expresses hope that his description of the plans will persuade Amphilochius to comply with his request.[66]

Very little is known about the life of Asterius of Amaseia. Using information gleaned from Asterius's homilies, Cornelis Datema estimates that he was born between 330 and 335 and educated by a Scythian slave of an Antiochian master—probably in Antioch itself—and that he lived in Chalcedon for a time, became bishop of Amaseia in Pontus sometime before 395 and died between 420 and 425.[67] This would mean that it was unlikely that Asterius knew Basil; there is no evidence that he knew the Gregorys personally, although this is possible. However, Asterius was greatly influenced by the thought and literary style of Gregory of Nyssa; several homilies, including his encomium on Stephen, demonstrate dependency on the works of the bishop of Nyssa.[68] His homilies also provide important information from this formerly Cappadocian area during and after the time of John Chrysostom's episcopate in Constantinople.

One thing all of these preachers agreed on was that the decisions of Nicea concerning the consubstantiality of the first two persons of the Trinity were correct. As we shall see, the two Gregorys and Asterius also taught the consubstantiality of the Holy Spirit, a position that was affirmed by the Council of Constantinople in 381. The involvement of these men in the theological, christological and pneumatological controversies of the time is reflected in all of their work, including their liturgical year homilies. One question we address in subsequent chapters is whether this involvement can be shown to have been directly *responsible* for any liturgical year developments, such as the adoption of Christmas or the appearance of a separate Feast of the Ascension forty days after Pascha.

Notes

1. Paul F. Bradshaw, *The Search for the Origins of Christian Worship: Sources and Methods for the Study of Early Liturgy* (New York: Oxford University Press, 1992), 65. Subsequent references will be cited as *Search*.
2. Much previous research into the Cappadocian liturgical year material has looked at individual slices of the data in order to trace the development of a particular Christian feast or season. Major works in this category include Hermann Usener, *Das Weihnachtsfest*, 3rd ed. (Bonn: H. Bouvier u. Co. Verlag, 1969); D. Bernard Botte, *Les origines de Noël et de l'Épiphanie*, Textes et études liturgiques 1 (Louvain: Abbaye du Mont César, 1932); Oscar Cullmann, *Noël dans l'Église ancienne*, Cahiers Théologiques de l'Actualité Protestante 25 (Neuchâtel: Delachaux & Niestlé, 1949); Justin Mossay, *Les fêtes de noël et de l'épiphanie d'après les sources Cappadociennes du IVe siècle* (Louvain: Abbaye du Mont César, 1965); Susan K. Roll, *Toward the Origins of Christmas* (Kampen, The Netherlands: Kok Pharos Publishing House, 1995); Robert Cabié, *La Pentecôte: l'évolution de la cinquantaine pascale au cours des cinq premiers siècles*, ed. A.-G. Martimort, Bibliothèque de Liturgie (Tournai: Desclée & Co., 1965); Hippolyte Delehaye, *Les Origines du Culte des Martyrs*, 2d rev. ed., Subsidia Hagiographica 20 (Brussels: Société des Bollandistes, 1933), 91; subsequent references to this last work will be

cited as *Origines*. Other scholars have included the Cappadocian material in their important works on the development of the liturgical year as a whole in the various Christian communities of the early period; see, for example, A. Allan McArthur, *The Evolution of the Christian Year* (Greenwich, Conn.: The Seabury Press, 1953); Thomas J. Talley, *The Origins of the Liturgical Year*, 2d ed. (Collegeville, MN: The Liturgical Press, 1991); subsequent references to this last work will be cited as *Origins*. Other scholars have produced shorter works on narrower aspects of the topic. These include Jean Daniélou, "Grégoire de Nysse et l'origine de la fête de l'Ascension," in *Kyriakon: Festschrift Johannes Quasten*, edited by Patrick Granfield and Josef A. Jungmann, 663–66 (Münster: Aschendorff, 1970); hereafter cited as "Grégoire"; Elie D. Moutsoulas, "Les sermons pascaux de Grégoire de Nysse," *Theologia* 51 (1980): 333–47; Robert L. Wilken, "Liturgy, Bible and Theology in the Easter Homilies of Gregory of Nyssa," in *Écriture et Culture Philosophique dans les Pensée de Grégoire de Nysse: Actes du Colloque de Chevetogne* (22–26 Septembre 1969), ed. Marguerite Harl, 127–43 (Leiden: E.J. Brill, 1971).

3. Between the reigns of Trajan (107–113) and Diocletian (284–305), Pontus was part of Cappadocia. Although they were separate provinces by the period under investigation, ties remained strong. For this reason and because the writings of Gregory of Nyssa strongly influenced his work, I have chosen to include the evidence from Asterius of Amaseia. In addition, Amphilochius became bishop of Iconium, which is in Lycaonia, but he himself was a Cappadocian and was strongly influenced by Basil.

4. I do not wish to draw too sharp a distinction between "episcopal" and "popular" viewpoints, as that has been shown to be a false, or at least overdrawn, dichotomy (Peter Brown, *The Cult of the Saints: Its Rise and Function in Latin Christianity*, The Haskell Lectures on History of Religions New Series No. 2, ed. Joseph M. Kitagawa [Chicago: The University of Chicago Press, 1981], 17ff.). My point is that if there were festal interpretations other than those that survive from these bishops, for the most part they remain unknown to us.

5. Where English translations of the homilies exist, they have been used, unless a more precise or literal translation was required. English translations of the remaining homilies have been prepared by the author for this study, using existing critical editions of the Greek texts. Unless otherwise noted, the translations are those of the author. For Basil, Greek texts of *Exhortatoria ad sanctum baptisma, In ebriosos, De jejunio I* and *II*, In *martyrem Julittam, In Gordium martyrem, In sanctos quadraginta martyres, In sanctum martyrem Mamantem* came from J.-P. Migne, ed, *Patrologiae Cursus Completus Series Græca*, vol. 31, (Paris: n.p., 1857); the text of *In sanctam Christi generationem* came from Saint Basil of Caesarea, *Opera omnia quae exstant vel quae ejus nomine circumferuntur*, ed. Julian Garnier, vol. 2, pt. 1 (Paris: Gaume Fratres, 1839). For Gregory of Nazianzus, the Greek text of *Oration* 44 came from J.-P. Migne, ed, *Patrologiae Cursus Completus Series Græca*, vol. 36, *Sancti Patris Nostri Gregorii Theologi Vulgo Nazianzeni, Archiepiscopi Constantinopolitani Opera Quae Exstant Omnia* (Paris: Migne, 1858). For Gregory of Nyssa, Greek texts for *In ascensionem Christi, In sanctam Pentecosten, In diem natalem salvatoris, In luciferam sanctam Domini resurrectionem, De sancto Theo-*

doro, In sanctum Stephanum I and *II, In XL martyres Ia, Ib* and *II* came from W.
Jaeger, *et al.*, eds., *Gregorii Nysseni Opera*, vol. 9, *Sermones, Pars I*, ed. Gunterus
Heil *et al.* (Leiden: E.J. Brill, 1967), vol. 10.1, *Sermones, Pars II,* ed. Gunterus Heil,
et al. (Leiden: E.J. Brill, 1967), and vol. 10.2, *Sermones, Pars III*, ed. Ernestus
Rhein, *et al.* (Leiden: E.J. Brill, 1996). For Amphilochius of Iconium, Greek texts
for *In natalitia Christi, In mesopentecosten* (spurious), *In diem Sabbati Sancti, De
recens baptizatis* came from E. Dekkers, *et al.*, gen. eds. *Corpus Christianorum*, Series Graeca, vol. 3, *Amphilochii Iconiensis Opera*, ed. Cornelis Datema (Turnout:
Brepols, 1978); references to the introductory material will be cited as Datema, *Amphilochius*. For Asterius of Amaseia, Greek texts for *Enarratio in martyrium praeclarissimae martyris Euphemiae, In S. Martyrem Phocam, Encomium in sanctos
martyres, Laudatio S. protomartyris Stephani, Oratio in principium jejuniorum*
came from C. Datema, ed., *Asterius of Amasea Homilies I–XIV: Text, Introduction
and Notes* (Leiden: E.J. Brill, 1970); references to the introductory material will be
cited as Datema, *Asterius*.

6.   Hereafter referred to as HM.
7.   Hippolyte Delehaye, "Martyrology," in *Catholic Encyclopedia*,
      http://www.newadvent.org/cathen/09741a.htm; hereafter cited as "Martyrology."
      See also I.B. De Rossi and L. Duchesne, eds., *Martyrologium Hieronymianum* (n.p.,
      n.d.), XLVI–LXXXI.
8.   Hereafter referred to as SM.
9.   W. Wright, "An Ancient Syrian Martyrology," *The Journal of Sacred Literature
      and Biblical Record* 8.15 (October 1865): 45; 8.16 (January 1866): 423–432.
10. Delehaye, "Martyrology" (Victor DeBuck, *Acta Sanctorum*, Octobris, XII, 185).
11. Delehaye, "Martyrology."
12. Delehaye, *Origines*, 91.
13. Hereafter referred to as *Typikon*.
14. Juan Mateos, ed. and trans., *Le Typicon de la Grande Église*, Orientalia Christiana
      Analecta 165, vol. 1, *Le Cycle des Douze Mois* (Rome: Pont. Institutum Orientalium
      Studiorum, 1962), xviii.
15. A English translation of Baumstark's original articulation of the method may be
      found in *Comparative Liturgy* (Westminster, MD, 1958).
16. Robert F. Taft, "Comparative Liturgy Fifty Years After Anton Baumstark (d. 1948):
      A Reply to Recent Critics," in *Worship* 73 (1999): 528.
17. Ibid., 522–523.
18. Bradshaw, *Search*, 62.
19. Robert Taft, "The Structural Analysis of Liturgical Units: An Essay in Methodol-
      ogy," in *Beyond East & West: Problems in Liturgical Understanding* (Washington,
      DC.: The Pastoral Press, 1984), 152–153.
20. Gregory of Nyssa, *In Basilium Fratrem*, W. Jaeger, *et al.*, eds., *Gregorii Nysseni
      Opera*, vol. 10.1, *Sermones*, part 2, ed. Gunterus Heil, *et al.* (Leiden: E.J. Brill,
      1967), 110.4–6. Where Richard (Casimir) McCambly's or my translations are used,
      subsequent references to Gregory's homilies will be cited as *GNO* by volume, page
      and line numbers, because there are no standard section numbers for Gregory's
      homilies.
21. Anthony Meredith, S.J., *The Cappadocians* (Crestwood, NY: St. Vladimir's Semi-

nary Press, 1995), 2. Subsequent references will be cited as *Cappadocians*.

22. A.H.M. Jones, *The Cities of the Eastern Roman Provinces*, 2d. ed. (Oxford: The Clarendon Press, 1971), 181–183.

23. Gregory of Nyssa, Letter 13 (*GNO*, Letter 17).

24. Interestingly, Tertullian (*Scorpiace* 12) quotes 1 Peter 2.20, saying that Peter was addressing the Christians of Pontus. Cyprian (*Testimonia ad Quirinium* 3.36, 37, 39) even refers to this letter as Peter's epistle to the people of Pontus.

25. Eusebius Pamphili, *Historia Ecclesiastica*, 3.1.

26. Ibid. 4.23.

27. Ibid. 5.23.

28. Tertullian, *Ad Scapulam* 3.

29. Anthony Meredith, S.J., *Gregory of Nyssa*, The Early Church Fathers Series, ed. Carol Harrison (London: Routledge, 1999), 1–2. Subsequent references will be cited as *Gregory*.

30. Eusebius Pamphili, *Historia Ecclesiastica*, 6.11.

31. Ibid. 7.28.1.

32. Meredith, *Cappadocians*, 3.

33. Basil of Caesarea, *On the Spirit* 29.74, *Nicene and Post-Nicene Fathers*, A Select Library of the Christian Church, Second Series, ed. Philip Schaff and Henry Wace (Grand Rapids: Wm. B. Eerdmans Publishing Company, 1954; reprint 1983), vol. 8, *St. Basil: Letters and Select Works*, 46–47; subsequent references to this series will be cited as *NPNF* by volume and page numbers.

34. Gregory of Nyssa, *Life of Gregory the Wonderworker* 3.27; 6.47.

35. Philip Rousseau, *Basil of Caesarea*, The Transformation of the Classical Heritage no. 20, ed. Peter Brown (Berkeley, CA: University of California Press, 1994), 4.

36. See below, p. 21. Firmilian tells an interesting story about a Cappadocian woman who was baptizing and celebrating the eucharist. His problem with her seems to have been more with her doctrinal errors than her sex.

37. Botte, *Origines*, 26.

38. For more complete biographical information, see Rousseau; also John A. McGuckin, *St. Gregory of Nazianzus: An Intellectual Biography* (Crestwood, NY: St. Vladimir's Seminary Press, 2001); Meredith, *Gregory of Nyssa*; Rosemary Radford Ruether, *Gregory of Nazianzus: Rhetor and Philosopher* (Oxford: The Clarendon Press, 1969); Gregory of Nazianzus, *De Vita Sua*; Datema, *Asterius of Amasea*.

39. The family estate was in Pontus, near Annisa. Basil was born either in Neocaesarea in Pontus or in Caesarea in Cappadocia (*NPNF*, Series 2, vol.8, xiii–xiv).

40. This Gregory was born in 329 or 330 either in Nazianzus or at Arianzus, a nearby country estate owned by his family. He died around 394.

41. Gregory of Nyssa, Letter 13.

42. The funeral oration for Basil given by Gregory of Nazianzus mentions that Basil encountered difficulty and opposition (*Or.* 43.37), and his letters give more information (see especially Letter 40). Basil and Gregory enlisted Gregory's father, the elderly bishop of Nazianzus, to help put Basil in the see of Caesarea, and they also involved Eusebius of faraway Samosata, which, as Rousseau points out, was probably less than canonically correct. Rousseau summarizes, "So we can detect already the indications that were likely to persist—quite apart from considerations of church

law (although, given the pressures against orthodoxy at the time, it is unlikely that Basil would have survived the imputation of any serious infringements). Unease about his care of the needy and the ascetic life, the underhand influence of family and friends, and a certain naivety (easily interpreted as arrogance) all would have prompted opposition" (Rousseau, 147).

43. Rousseau, 7.

44. Basil of Caesarea, Letter 58, *Saint Basil Letters: Volume I (1–185)*, trans. Agnes Clare Way, C.D.P, *The Fathers of the Church*, ed. Roy Joseph Deferrari *et al.* (New York: Fathers of the Church, Inc., 1955), 149; subsequent references to these two volumes of translations of Basil's letters will be cited as *FOTC* and by letter, volume and page numbers.

45. Basil of Caesarea, Letters 59 and 60.

46. Raymond Van Dam, "Emperor, Bishops, and Friends in Late Antique Cappadocia," *The Journal of Theological Studies* n.s. 37 (1986), 66.

47. Basil of Caesarea, Letter 100.

48. Van Dam, 69. See Gregory of Nazianzus, *Or.* 10.2; 11.3; 12.4; *Epistle* 63.6.

49. Ruether, 180.

50. Gregory of Nazianzus, *Concerning His Own Life* 440–463, in *The Fathers of the Church: A New Translation*, ed. Thomas P. Halton *et al.*, vol. 75, *Saint Gregory of Nazianzus: Three Poems*, trans. Denis Molaise Meehan (Washington, D.C., 1987), 89–90; subsequent references to this volume will be cited as *FOTC* by section and page numbers.

51. Ibid. 384–399, *FOTC*, 75, 88.

52. See Basil of Caesarea, Letter 150.

53. The famine that struck Cappadocia in 369 was probably the main impetus behind Basil's construction of the *Basileiados*, a complex of medical and food distribution facilities, residences (for the bishop, guests and patients), workshops and a church, all located just outside Caesarea (Rousseau, 139–140). Basil's Letter 94 to Elias, Governor of Cappadocia, is a defense against criticism of this complex. In the letter from "Heracleidas," Basil makes a connection between this project and his own non-eremitic form of asceticism.

54. Basil of Caesarea, Letter 150.

55. Iconium was not a Cappadocian city; in this period it was located in the province of Lycaonia. Amphilochius's homilies, therefore, do not necessarily reflect *Cappadocian* practice. They are included in this study because Amphilochius was a native of Cappadocia, a relative of Gregory of Nazianzus and a protégé of Basil; in fact, Basil's influence on Amphilochius was great. Amphilochius's homilies, therefore, may reflect the spread of Cappadocian practice to nearby areas.

56. Rousseau, 258.

57. Basil of Caesarea, Letters 200–202, 232.

58. Ibid., Letters 233–236.

59. Rousseau, 260. Apparently, the area was troubled not only by theological disagreements, but also by "unruliness" and "brigandage" such as banditry and rebellions (John Matthews, *The Roman Empire of Ammianus* [Baltimore: The Johns Hopkins University Press, 1989], 355–367).

60. Gregory of Nazianzus, Letter 63.6.

61. Ibid., Letter 1.
62. Ibid., Letters 72–74.
63. Ibid., Letters 76, 182 and 197, respectively.
64. Ibid., Letters 9, 25–28, 171, 184.
65. Ibid., Letter 171.
66. Gregory of Nyssa, Letter 16.
67. Datema, *Asterius*, xix–xxiv.
68. Ibid., xxiii.

Chapter 2

The Paschal Cycle

This chapter on the paschal cycle of the fourth/early fifth-century Cappadocian liturgical year will attempt to answer several questions. First, we must address a matter of prehistory in order to ascertain as clearly as possible the paschal practice from which the fourth-century Cappadocian calendar developed; were the churches of Cappadocia among the communities in Asia Minor that prior to the Council of Nicea observed the Pascha on 14 Nisan, or on as close an approximation of that date as they could calculate? Second, in the time period on which we are focusing, is there evidence from Cappadocia of a multi-day but unitive Pascha breaking down into discreet commemorations of Christ's crucifixion and burial on Friday, repose in the tomb on Saturday and resurrection on Saturday night/Sunday morning? Third, is there evidence of a unitive *season* of Pentecost disintegrating into separate feasts of Pascha and its Octave, Ascension and *day* of Pentecost? Fourth, did the Cappadocian churches of this period observe Lent? If so, how was it arranged and what purposes did it serve?

Quartodeciman Pascha

Early evidence from Asia Minor shows that, for many second-century Christian communities in the region, Pascha was a vigil kept during the night of 14/15 Nisan (the Jewish Passover) that lasted beyond the conclusion of Passover and ended with celebration of the eucharist at dawn.[1] This Pascha was the commemoration of Christ's death,[2] but as Talley points out, "...this death is not seen as merely one incident in an extended Holy Week scenario. Rather, the content of the celebration is the entire work of redemption: the incarnation, the passion, the resurrection and glorification, all focused upon the Cross as locus of Christ's triumph."[3] These communities observed Pascha on Passover, but because they were so far from Palestine, it was difficult for them to determine precisely when Passover began. Talley describes the problem succinctly:

The inadequacy of the Jewish calendar, whose twelve lunar months did not equal a solar year, presented difficulties for the maintenance of uniform practice. This was a problem even for Jews in the diaspora, since in the second century no system was yet established for the intercalation of an added month when the disparity with the solar year became too great, and necessary adjustments were made ad hoc. In the second century a letter was sent out from the sages of Palestine to Jews in the diaspora ordering an additional month for that year.... Nonetheless, such measures often failed to preserve unity of observance. Whatever problem the date of Passover presented for Jews, it must have been even more of a problem for Asian Christians who believed that they must observe Pascha on the fourteenth day of the first month. Christians were separated from the synagogues by the end of the first century, and were thereafter independent of the rabbinical authorities who determined the adjustment of the calendar by the periodic addition of an intercalary month. Apart from that authority, Christians could not know which month was first. Further, they lived in a culture that followed the solar Julian calendar and had done so since 9 B.C.[4]

Despite this difficulty, it was imperative for Quartodeciman communities to figure out precisely when the fourteenth day of the first month was, so that they could observe Pascha on what they believed was the actual anniversary of Christ's crucifixion; for this reason, Asian Christians abandoned the Palestinian rabbinical lunar calendar, adopted the Asian recension of the Julian solar calendar and celebrated Pascha on the fourteenth day of the first spring month according to the calendar being used in their region.[5]

Were the churches of Cappadocia among these Quartodecimans? Communities in many other regions of Asia Minor were Quartodeciman; there is evidence from Sardis, Ephesus, Laodicea, Hieropolis, and Smyrna.[6] Eusebius claims that this was the tradition of "all Asia." He writes:

Now, at this time, no small controversy was stirred up because the dioceses of all Asia, as according to an older tradition, thought that they should observe the fourteenth day of the moon, on which the Jews had been ordered to sacrifice the lamb, as the feast of the Saviour's Passover, so that it became absolutely necessary to bring the days of fasting to an end on whatever day of the week this fell. But it was not the custom for the churches throughout the rest of the world to end it in this way, since they preserved a custom which from apostolic tradition has prevailed to our own day, according to which it is not right to end the fasting on any other day than that of the Resurrection of our Saviour. Then, synods and conferences of bishops on the same question took place, and they unanimously formulated in their letters a doctrine of the Church for people everywhere, that the mystery of the Lord's Resurrection from the dead be celebrated on no other day than the Lord's Day, and that on this day alone we should observe the close of the Paschal fast.[7]

Among the synods that met in the late second century to address this question and to declare that the annual celebration of Christ's resurrection should take place on a Sunday, Eusebius lists a meeting of the bishops of Pontus, presided over by Palmas, who was Bishop of Amestris in the last quarter of the second century. The fact that a synod was necessary to settle the matter indicates that it was indeed an issue for this area, but we have no specific information about the rest of Cappadocia in this period. Firmilian, bishop of Caesarea in Cappadocia in the middle of the third century, corresponded with Cyprian of Carthage about several controverted issues, including the rebaptism of those originally baptized by heretics. In a letter written in 256, he refers to the variety of practices concerning Easter:

> But that they who are at Rome do not observe those things in all cases which are handed down from the beginning, and vainly pretend the authority of the apostles; any one may know also from the fact, that concerning the celebration of Easter, and concerning many other sacraments of divine matters, he may see that there are some diversities among them, and that all things are not observed among them alike, which are observed at Jerusalem, just as in very many other provinces also many things are varied because of the difference of the places and names.[8]

Unfortunately, Firmilian does not say whether one of the variations of practice in his province concerned the day on which to celebrate Easter, but it is tempting to speculate so, given his disapproving tone about Rome's assumption of authority in this matter.

Despite the synods of the second century, the controversy over the calculation of the date of Easter persisted into the fourth century. In 325 the Council of Nicea attempted to impose uniformity of practice by legislating that the Alexandrian method of determining the date of Easter be followed. Nicea also adopted March 21 as the date of the spring equinox, as the Alexandrians observed.[9] Nicea also may have prohibited the practice of celebrating the Pascha before the spring equinox, but as Anscar Chupungco notes, "Some Church Fathers claimed that the Council of Nicea sanctioned this canon, but the conciliar document on the matter, if there had been any, is irretrievably lost."[10] Also, at the conclusion of the Council, Constantine sent a letter to the churches of the Roman world directing: "Then also, when there was a question about the most holy day of the Pascha, it was decided by common accord that it would be well for everyone everywhere to celebrate on the same day.... And firstly it seemed unsuitable that we should celebrate that holy festival following the custom of the Jews...."[11]

The bishops gathered at Nicea, therefore, addressed two main concerns in their deliberations over the date of the celebration of the Pascha: that it be observed on the same day in all regions of the Christian world[12] and that the calculations of both the equinox and the date of the Paschal observance be different from those of the Jews. Uniformity among Christians and distance from the Jews were the issues, and not, as Chupungco correctly points out, making sure that the Pascha was celebrated on a Sunday.[13]

The decisions of Nicea apparently did not solve the problem. As Chupungco notes, "Nevertheless, this decision did not put an end to variation, since some groups of Christians persisted in their traditional customs, and in any case no particular table to compute the date of Easter appears to have been prescribed by Constantine."[14] In Constantine's letter to the churches following the Council of Nicea, which is recorded in Eusebius's *Vita Constantini*, the dioceses of Asia and Pontus are included in the long list of regions that observed Easter as Rome and Alexandria did.[15] If this is true, then in post-Nicene Cappadocia, Pascha was celebrated on Saturday night/Sunday morning as it was in most of the rest of the churches. However, Epiphanius, bishop of Salamis on the northeast coast of Cyprus from 367 to 403, tells us that Quartodeciman Christians inhabited Cappadocia a half a century after the Council of Nicea. In his *Panarion haereseon*, written in the 370s, he writes:

> 1,3 The Quartodecimans contentiously keep the Passover on one day, once a year, even though their doctrine of the Father, the Son and the Holy Spirit is good and in agreement with <ours>, and they accept the prophets, apostles and evangelists, and likewise confess the resurrection of the flesh and the coming judgment, and everlasting life. (4) But they have fallen into an error, and one of no small importance, by following the letter, if you please, of the Law's saying, "Cursed is he who shall not keep the Passover on the fourteenth day of the month." (5) Others though, who keep the same one day and fast and celebrate the mysteries on the same one day, boast that they have found the precise date in the Acts of Pilate, if you please; it says there that the Savior suffered on the eighth before the Kalends of April.
>
> 1,6 They keep the Passover on whichever day it is that the fourteenth of the month falls; but the ones in Cappadocia keep the same one day on the eighth before the Kalends of April. (7) And there is no little dissension in their ranks, since some say the fourteenth day of the month, but some, the eighth before the Kalends of April. (8) Furthermore, I have found copies of the Acts of Pilate which say that the passion came on the fifteenth before the Kalends of April. But in fact, as I know from much minute investigation, I have found that the Savior suffered on the thirteenth before the Kalends of April. Some, however, say it was the tenth before the Kalends of April.[16]

So, according to Epiphanius, "the ones in Cappadocia" (οἱ ἐν τῇ Καππα-δοκίᾳ) observed the Pascha on the eighth before the kalends of April (March 25), which corresponded to 14 Teireix, the first month of spring on the Cappadocian calendar.[17] This means that, according to Epiphanius, even in the last quarter of the fourth century absolute uniformity regarding the date of Easter still did not exist. As we will see later in this chapter, most Christians were observing a forty-day Lent, a Triduum, and a Sunday Easter. However, if Epiphanius's information is accurate, at least a few Cappadocian Christians observed the Pascha on one day—the day calculated to be the anniversary of Christ's passion. Is it possible that Nyssa was one of these pockets of resistance?

One of Gregory of Nyssa's paschal homilies contains a puzzling but tantalizing discussion related to this question. In *On the Three-Day Period of the Resurrection of our Lord Jesus Christ*, he says:

> But it would be proper to include briefly in the discussion the points made by the Jews in disparaging attacks on our principles. They say that in the paschal text the Jews have had appointed by Moses the fourteenth period in the lunar cycle and the eating of unleavened bread for seven days, and that as a relish for the unleavened bread they should prepare a dish of bitter herbs. "If then you are careful about the observance of the fourteenth day," says the Jew, "then the bitters and the unleavened bread should be observed at the same time; and if the latter are not worth keeping, why bother about the former? For when it is the same lawgiver, one thing is not judged just and edifying and another useless and to be rejected; so it follows that either all that was laid down about the pascha should be kept by you, or you should not retain any." What do we say to that? Let us remember the exhortation not to be daunted by human insult nor to succumb to their denigration. For we know what is edifying about the unleavened bread and the benefit of the bitter herbs and the benefit of the fourteenth day.[18]

What are we to make of this reference to the observance of the fourteenth day in a homily delivered at least sixty years after the Council of Nicea?[19] Chupungco, assuming that the Jews in question were not simply a rhetorical device, suggests that they were either confusing Gregory's Sunday-observing community with the small pockets of Quartodecimans still existing in the fourth century or referring to those who used 14 Nisan in their calculations to determine the date of Easter Sunday. He also maintains that Gregory's answer shows that he is speaking on a purely symbolic level when he claims to observe the fourteenth; Chupungco writes, "14 Nisan has meaning for Christians in so far as it symbolizes renewal of life."[20]

This may very well be the case. In answering the Jews, Gregory spiritualizes the Mosaic Law. He explains that the law "contains the shadow of good things to come" and "is aimed at one principal end, which is that man should be purified by its various injunctions from the evil infused in his nature."[21] He then spiritualizes circumcision, Sabbath observance, dietary laws, and feast-keeping and explains that the seven days represent a person's life, which is made up of a series of seven-day periods. The fourteenth day of the lunar cycle (which Gregory says lasts 29 ½ days) is the day when there is no darkness, because the full moon appears before the sun sets and remains until sunrise the next day. For Gregory this symbolizes the life of the virtuous person, which is flavored by chastity and not contaminated by works of darkness. The continuous light in the heavens on this day is "a symbol for those who celebrate spiritually, so that throughout the week of their life they may accomplish one pascha, luminous and undarkened for the whole period in which they live." Gregory then explains:

> This is for Christians what constitutes the paschal commandments. We thus look at the fourteenth and obtain through this perceptible and material light the impression of the immaterial and intelligible, so that while we apparently seek a full moon which provides us with the light which it gives to last the whole night long, yet in reality our law requires us to take care that all the time that is measured by night and day should be continuously bright, and free from admixture of the works of darkness.[22]

However, it is also possible that we should interpret Gregory's words about the fourteenth literally. Anthony Meredith makes an important observation; he points out that if Gregory's community celebrated Pascha on a Sunday, he would not have had to resort to such a complex explanation. Meredith writes:

> It could of course be argued that the expression 'fourteenth day' simply means Easter Sunday, and that to suggest that Gregory kept any other type of Easter is to press the language too closely. It should also be remembered that the Canons of the Council of Nicaea had explicitly forbidden the observance of Easter on the Jewish date.... Nevertheless this does not of itself lead us to the conclusion that we must interpret the text of Gregory to mean that the fourteenth day equals Easter. If that is all it meant it would, surely, have been possible for him to reply that Christians did not observe the date of the fourteenth Nisan, and finish with the argument there.... First of all, the status of the Council was not quite so clear to contemporaries as it became to later generations.... There seems therefore to be no compelling reason for

ruling out the possibility that Christians in Cappadocia observed the fourteenth Nisan well on into the fourth century.[23]

Gregory himself seems to corroborate this interpretation of his meaning. In a letter to Eusebius of Chalcis, he explains why Christmas and Pascha occur in their respective seasons of the year. In addition, using language very similar to that of the homily, he explains why Pascha happens at the full moon. He writes:

> But the feast of the Resurrection, occurring when the days are of equal length, of itself gives us this interpretation of the coincidence, namely, that we shall no longer fight with evils only upon equal terms, vice grappling with virtue in indecisive strife, but that the life of light will prevail, the gloom of idolatry melting as the day waxes stronger. For this reason also, after the moon has run her course for fourteen days, Easter exhibits her exactly opposite to the rays of the sun, full with all the wealth of his brightness, and not permitting any interval of darkness to take place in its turn: for, after taking the place of the sun at its setting, she does not herself set, before she mingles her own beams with the genuine rays of the sun, so that one light remains continuously, throughout the whole space of the earth's course by day and night, without any break whatsoever being caused by the interposition of darkness.[24]

If Gregory means that his community celebrated Pascha on the fourteenth, to which fourteenth is he referring? Is the community one of "the ones in Cappadocia" discussed by Epiphanius, who celebrated Pascha on the eighth before the kalends of April, 14 Teireix? I do not think so. Both the homily and the letter in question rely heavily on the coincidence of Pascha and the full moon. Since the Cappadocian calendar was not a lunar calendar, 14 Teireix would not always fall on the full moon. The only fourteenth day guaranteed to always fall on the full moon is 14 Nisan. So Gregory's discussions are either entirely symbolic or his was a community still resisting the Nicene paschal legislation. As Meredith says, "because Nicea said so" is not a good enough reason to rule out the latter possibility. Based on these excerpts from Gregory's work, it is possible that his community at Nyssa was a Quartodeciman, although not the kind Epiphanius knew.

Disintegration of a Unitive Pascha?

Whether or not Gregory of Nyssa's community was Quartodeciman, his extant paschal sermons do not display the kind of differentiation among the days of the Triemeron that is evident in the sermons of Gregory of Nazianzus and Amphilochius, although we do note some ambiguity. On the one hand, the Pascha is the day of resurrection. In *Discourse on the Holy Pascha*, composed in 382,[25] Gregory exhorts his listeners, "Let us speak of the things proper to the feast, so that we may celebrate in a way corresponding and naturally fitting to its subject-matter."[26] The first item on the agenda is celebrating the resurrection of Christ. In addition, we not only remember and celebrate *Christ's* resurrection on "this day," we also *anticipate* our own future resurrections, which are made possible by what we celebrate today.[27] On the other hand, Gregory's homilies also contain traces of the idea of Pascha as a multi-themed unity, perhaps encompassing several days. In his *In luciferam sanctam Domini resurrectionem* Gregory exhorts his congregation, "Therefore, let us celebrate a three-day period (τριήμερον) producing resurrection of eternal life."[28] If this "three-day period" refers to the feast itself, this would be strong evidence *against* the conclusion that Gregory's community was Quartodeciman, since the Quartodeciman paschal observance lasted only one day. However, the rest of the sermon makes it clear that Gregory is exhorting his congregation to commemorate a past event that took place over a period of three days. In other words, "three-day period" refers to the historical event being celebrated, not to the celebration itself. His *On the Three-Day Period of the Resurrection of our Lord Jesus Christ* also presents a multi-themed paschal vigil. The sermon is not entirely about Christ's resurrection, although that is certainly one of its themes. He describes the light-filled church, illuminated by "a multitude of candles." He uses this light as a metaphor for "the whole blessing of Christ, shining by itself like a torch"—a light that is constituted by "the many and varied rays of scripture." He then focuses on several of these "rays" as "divinely inspired examples" of "what is appropriate to the present holy season" (ἡ παροῦσα ἱερομηνία).[29]

What does Gregory of Nyssa consider appropriate to this particular holy season? Baptism is the first thing he mentions. More specifically, he sees in the neophytes the fulfillment of God's promises to give Abraham innumerable descendents, referring to them as "these stars which have just risen upon us through the Spirit and have made the church all at once a heaven."[30]

The second appropriate theme is Christ's repose in the tomb, which Gregory discusses in terms of sabbath:

> For on this day the only begotten God truly rested from all his works, having kept sabbath in the flesh through the dispensation befitting death, and returning to what he was by his resurrection he raised again together with himself all that lay pros-

trate, becoming life and resurrection and sunrise and dawn and day for those in darkness and death's shadow.[31]

Abraham's offering up of Isaac supplies a third example; Jesus is both the beloved son being offered and the lamb provided to be the offering in his stead (Gen. 22). Moses prefigures the cross with his own body when he stretches out his arms and defeats the Amalekite.[32] Isaiah's contribution was his prediction of the virgin birth, and Jonah's three-day stay in the belly of the whale prophesied the Lord's sojourn in Hades.[33]

Gregory then moves into a discussion of the unique nature of Pascha. These and similar passages from the Hebrew scriptures depend on "the present brightness," which has changed everything and inaugurated a new creation. This day unlike any other day "undid the pain of death, this was midwife to the firstborn from the dead, in it the iron gates of death were crushed, in it the brazen bars of Hades were shattered."[34]

Thus, Gregory's paschal vigil sermon that year was illuminated by several scriptural "rays" making up the torch of the blessing of Christ—baptism and the neophytes as fulfillment of promise, Christ's repose in the tomb, sacrifice, and Pascha as inauguration of the new creation. This sermon also contains reflections on a three-day period, but again he is clearly referring to the three days from Christ's passion to his resurrection, not to the three days from Good Friday to Easter Sunday. He answers several questions. First, why did it happen? Jesus chose to do it in order to defeat Satan and death. Essentially, God tricked Satan:

> For since it was impossible for the prince of darkness to engage with the presence of the Light having observed no portion of flesh in him, when he saw the Godbearing flesh and saw also the miracles done through it by the deity, he consequently hoped that, if he were to seize the flesh through death, he would also get hold of all the power in it. For this reason, having swallowed the bait of the flesh, he was pierced with the fishhook of deity....[35]

In defeating Satan, Christ also defeated evil and death, which Gregory says are "the things which the 3-day space of time has achieved for you."[36]

The next question Gregory addresses is "Why did it take so long?" His response is that three days was actually a very *short* time in which to accomplish the defeat of evil and restoration of millions of human souls. In addition, the supreme power of Christ is manifested in the fact that he accomplished this work in such a quiet way, not with flood or flame but through "a simple and incomprehensible visit, a mere coming of Life and Light...."[37]

Gregory then suggests that the number of days corresponded to the number of evils that needed to be remedied. "Evil had a three-fold genesis." It originated in the serpent, defeated the woman and then defeated the man. "Since therefore evil abounded in these three, I mean the diabolic nature and the race of women and the multitude of men, consequently the disease is abolished in three consecutive days, one day being allotted to the healing of each kind of those infected with evil."[38]

Gregory then notes that the passion, death, burial and resurrection of Christ did *not*, in fact, take three full days and asks why it is referred to as a three-day period. First, he begins the counting of the days on Thursday evening, not Friday, because the salvific three days began when Jesus offered himself, not when Judas betrayed him or the Jews captured him or Pilate condemned him. Gregory's second strategy concerns the Friday of the crucifixion. Because of the unusual noontime darkness reported in Matthew 27.45, he claims that that particular Friday was, in fact, two days. He interprets Matthew 28.1 to mean that the resurrection took place "late on the sabbath." So Gregory calculates the three days, adding for good measure that God is not bound by human time anyway:

> If this is the way these things are, our interval lasts from Thursday evening to the (290) Saturday evening, measuring separately the time of the extra night which, as we said, chops the Friday into two days and one night. For it was right in the case of the [*sic*] him who rules the temporal order by his sovereign power that his works should not necessarily be forced to fit set measures of time, but that the measures of time should be newly contrived for what his works required, and that as the divine power accomplishes good actions more expeditiously, the measures of time should just be shortened, in such a way that the time should be reckoned not less than three days and the same number of nights, since that was the number required by the mystical and ineffable reasoning (logos); and so that the divine power should not be impeded in the speed of its performance through waiting for the normal divisions of days and nights. For the one who has power both to lay down his life of his own accord and to take it again had power when he wished as creator of the temporal orders not to be bound by time for his actions, but to create time to fit his actions.[39]

Gregory's explanation may be labored and, in any case, is intended largely to force the scripture to make sense when perhaps it does not. However, his argument is instructive for our purposes as well, since it treats the days of the original Triemeron as a unity and perhaps indicates that the annual observance of the days was also still a unity in Nyssa at this time. On the other hand, it could represent a reaction on his part to a perceived separation of the days, as was happening in Nazianzus and Iconium.

Thomas K. Carroll and Thomas Halton state that "Holy Saturday, for the most part, had no distinctive and proper liturgy in the early Church and this very vacuity in itself symbolized the repose of the tomb." To support this observation, they cite Gregory of Nyssa's *De tridui spatio*, which, as mentioned above, was composed for a paschal vigil but is dominated by the themes of Sabbath and repose.[40] Another of Gregory of Nyssa's paschal vigil homilies, *The Holy and Saving Pascha*,[41] also contains an oblique reference to the events of Holy Saturday:

> The true Sabbath rest, the one which received God's benediction, in which the Lord rested from his own works by keeping sabbath for the world's salvation in the inactivity of death, has now reached its goal and has displayed its own grace alike to eyes and ears and heart, through all those features of the festival solemnized among us by which we have seen, by which we have heard, by which we have welcomed joy to the heart. The light seen by our eyes was torch-lit for us in the night by the cloud of fire from our candles. The night-long word resounding in our hearing with psalms and hymns and spiritual songs (Col. 3,16), like some flood of happiness pouring into the soul through our ears, has made us full of good hopes.[42]

By this time, in many other regions of the Roman Empire, the Pascha *had* begun to be broken down into distinct days, each with a different piece of the passion/resurrection narrative as its theme. Cantalamessa maintains that this was due to a "process of historicizing the paschal mystery" and appears to have happened most clearly and rapidly in the East, noting the Cappadocian Fathers and *Apostolic Constitutions* as evidence for Asia Minor and Syria; Egeria and the Armenian Lectionary show a similar trend in Jerusalem. Cantalamessa writes:

> The predominant criterion here is no longer that of the mystery but that of the history: not to celebrate the whole mystery of Christ synthetically but to celebrate each event at the time—and, at Jerusalem, in the very place—of its original occurrence. This historicized Pascha quickly leads to the paschal cycle of feasts. In fact it is from this region that we have the first witnesses to the distinct feasts of the Descent into Hell on Holy Saturday..., the Octave of Easter..., the Ascension, and Pentecost Sunday.... The evolution is more visible than ever precisely in the two key terms *pascha* and *pentêkostês*: the former comes to mean ever more frequently the Sunday of the Resurrection, while the latter comes to refer to the feast of the Holy Spirit celebrated on the fiftieth day....[43]

Since Gregory Dix's classic articulation of the "history vs. eschatology" model,[44] this has become the standard interpretation of the data about late-fourth-century paschal practice. Does the evidence from Cappadocia support it? Gregory of Nyssa's sermons do not, but other post-Nicene sources from Cappadocia do indicate an embryonic paschal cycle. In some of the data, Pascha clearly refers to the "day of resurrection." In an oration delivered on Easter 362, the first Easter after he was ordained to the priesthood, Gregory of Nazianzus says: "It is the Day of the Resurrection, and my Beginning has good auspices. Let us then keep the Festival with splendour, and let us embrace one another." He continues, "A Mystery anointed me; I withdrew a little while at a Mystery, as much as was needful to examine myself; now I come in with a Mystery, bringing with me the Day as a good defender of my cowardice and weakness; that He Who to-day rose again from the dead may renew me also by His Spirit...."[45] However, in this oration, Gregory also contrasts the "today" of deliverance, glorification and resurrection with the "yesterday" of the Passover, crucifixion, death and burial. He says:

> Yesterday the lamb was slain and the doorposts were anointed, and Egypt bewailed her firstborn, and the Destroyer passed us over, and the Seal was dreadful and awesome, and we were walled in with the "precious blood" (1 Pet 1:19). Today we have clean escaped from Egypt and from our harsh master, the Pharaoh, and from the oppressive overseers, and we have been freed from the mortar and the brick, and there is no one to keep us from celebrating a feast to the Lord our God—the feast of departure—and from feasting, not "with the old leaven of wickedness and depravity but with the unleavened bread of sincerity and truth" (1 Cor 5:8), bringing with us none of the godless Egyptian dough.
>
> Yesterday I was crucified with Christ, today I am glorified with him; yesterday I died with him, today I am brought to life with him; yesterday I was buried with him, today I am raised up with him.[46]

Are these literal references to what yesterday was "about" and what today is about? Cantalamessa notes that in the eleventh century Nicetas of Heraclea claimed that by "yesterday" Gregory meant Lent in this homily. Cantalamessa disagrees:

> But it is more likely that Gregory only wishes to contrast Good Friday and Holy Saturday with Easter Sunday. In any case, here, as in Basil..., we see how the Church has begun to distribute the content of the Pascha over several days. The term *Pascha* continues to designate the fast, vigil, and Eucharist of the night before Sunday, but in this liturgy the moment of the Cross is now greatly attenuated in favor of the Resurrection....[47]

Cantalamessa maintains that this distinction between the days of passion and resurrection is new with this sermon.[48] According to Wolfgang Huber, this distinction reveals not only the historicization of Pascha but also an anti-Arian elevation of the resurrection over the passion in an attempt to reject the notion that Christ's humanity was in any way weak or that it in any way detracted from his divinity and omnipotence.[49]

In another paschal oration, composed twenty or thirty years later, Gregory continues to differentiate among the days, but he also blurs festal distinctions. The day for which this oration was composed is clearly the day celebrating Christ's resurrection, distinct even, perhaps, from the paschal vigil. He says:

> The Lord's Passover, the Passover, and again I say the Passover to the honour of the Trinity! This is to us a Feast of feasts and a Solemnity of solemnities as far exalted above all others (not only those which are merely human and creep on the ground, but even those which are of Christ Himself, and are celebrated in His honour) as the Sun is above the stars. Beautiful indeed yesterday was our splendid array, and our illumination, in which both in public and private we associated ourselves, every kind of men, and almost every rank, illuminating the night with our crowded fires, formed after the fashion of that great light, both that with which the heaven above us lights its beacon fires, and that which is above the heavens, amid the angels (the first luminous nature, next to the first nature of all, because springing directly from it), and that which is in the Trinity, from which all light derives its being, parted from the undivided light and honoured.
>
> But today's is more beautiful and more illustrious; inasmuch as yesterday's light was forerunner of the rising of the Great Light, and as it were a kind of rejoicing in preparation for the Festival, but today we are celebrating the Resurrection itself, no longer as an object of expectation, but as having already come to pass, and gathering the whole world unto itself.[50]

However, Gregory's main purpose is to demonstrate how the definitive redemptive work of Christ in the passion and resurrection fits into the whole of salvation history; this work depended upon Christ's having been born in the first place ("...my present subject is not the doctrine of God but that of the Incarnation").[51] For this reason, he expands the festal agenda:

> Such is the feast thou art keeping today, and in this manner I would have thee celebrate both the Birthday and the Burial of Him who was born for thee and suffered for thee. Such is the Mystery of the Passover; such are the mysteries sketched by the Law and fulfilled by Christ, the Abolisher of the letter, the Perfecter of the Spirit, who by His Passion taught us how to suffer, and by His glorification grants us to be glorified with Him.[52]

Gregory also brings in themes that we would associate with Good Friday and Holy Saturday—and even the Ascension![53] This sounds more like Talley's description of second-century Pascha as celebration of the whole work of redemption than Catalamessa's picture of the fourth-century historicized Pascha, but it more likely reflects Gregory's homiletical agenda to preach right belief about the nature and plan of God, especially concerning the incarnation.

Other evidence makes it clear that the disintegration process is underway. In a letter to Helladius, Gregory of Nazianzus refers to "the holy day of the Pascha (τὴν ἁγίαν τοῦ Πάσχα ἡμέραν)."[54] During his episcopate at Caesarea, Basil describes Pascha as the most suitable—though not only—time for baptism; in so doing, he refers to it as the "day of resurrection":

> On the one hand, therefore, [there is] a different time suitable to different things; one proper to sleep, one proper to waking; one proper to war, one proper to peace; but the time for baptism, on the other hand, [is] the whole life of humans.... Therefore, on the one hand, every time is an opportune time for salvation through baptism.... But, on the other hand, perhaps it is reasonable to many that the more proper time is the more suitable time. But what would be more natural than the day of the Pascha for baptism?[55]

It is from nearby Iconium that we first see Holy Saturday clearly emerging as a day with its own content. Amphilochius's *In diem Sabbati Sancti*[56] contains our earliest clear evidence for Holy Saturday as a liturgical observance of Christ's burial and descent into hell.[57] Amphilochius says:

> Today we celebrate a burial feast of our savior. On the one hand, he is the one who both dissolves the bonds of death among the dead below and fills Hades with light and wakes those who have died from sleep, but we, on the other hand, dance above the earth, as we imagine the resurrection, and we have not feared corruption, lest it win a victory over incorruptibility.[58]

He also distinguishes between Holy Saturday and Good Friday. Using the same yesterday/today construction that Gregory of Nazianzus uses in *Oration 1*, Amphilochius contrasts the two days:

> Yesterday he dimmed the sun when he was crucified, and when it was the middle of the day, night rushed in; today death is undone, because it welcomed a dead man who was foreign to it. Yesterday the creation mourned when it saw the madness of the Jews and put on the darkness like a mourning garment; today 'the people sitting in darkness have seen a great light.' Yesterday the earth was shaken and considered

fleeing and threatened to separate from those who dwell [on it]; and the mountains mourned, and the rocks were split, and the temple was stripped bare....[59]

Amphilochius also anticipates "the third day," on which the atrocities of the crucifixion and the absurdities of the burial will be answered. He says, "Resurrection is not hindered by arms, it is not fettered by seals, it is not prevented by soldiers, it is not stolen by money."[60] He also takes his listeners right up to the last moment before the risen Christ reveals his identity to Mary; immediately before a trinitarian doxology, Amphilochius exhorts them to imagine themselves at the tomb with Mary, saying "They have taken our Lord away, and we do not know what they have done with him."[61]

Amphilochius reserves most of his resurrection rhetoric for that third day; his oration *De recens baptizatis*[62] is a beautiful meditation on the splendors of the day of resurrection. The opening section describes the sweetness of spring as it replaces the "gloominess of winter" with many-colored birds singing sweet-sounding songs and with refreshing breezes reviving the plants. Amphilochius concludes, "And, beloved, the earthly and perishable spring supplies this delight to humans, but Christ, our divine and undefiled spring, having covered the meadow of the church with the faith of spiritual violets and roses and lilies, makes the vision bright and fills the reservoir of our heart with divine spices."[63]

The lovely visual and olfactory imagery continues as Amphilochius rejoices over the newly baptized Christians in their midst:

> For who of the faithful does not now rejoice? And who does not now rejoice when he sees the neophytes, shining in an image of lilies with the radiant ornaments of the robes and having gained the faith that shines like gold in the middle of the heart? Here you will find, beloved, having looked intently with the eyes of the heart, in the manner of a deepest violet, the heart of the faithful being purplish with the blood of Jesus; for the flame-leafed rose purely put forth a flower from the virgin Mary. What kind of meadow [is] our meadow that has gained such a sweet smell as the spicing grace of the spirit? Catch the scent of the neophyte, and you will find in him the immortal sweet smell of the spirit, indeed I speak of the oil (μύρον) of the heavenly anointing (χρίσματος). Here the palm trees of the father, wreathed with the palm branches of victory, bloom the sweeter fruits of love; here the beautiful-sounding birds of the psalmists play the psalms to God with one voice on the lyre; here virginity rejoices in the manner of storax, carrying the pure incense of prayer to God; here moderation fully enjoys itself, sacrificing to God the joyous branch of strict observance of religious duties as Abraham [did] Isaac; here the roots of mercies, putting forth the branch of beneficence to the poor, on the one hand, delight the Lord and, on the other hand, nourish the beggar.[64]

In addition to providing information about baptismal practice, Amphilochius also gives us glimpses of other parts of the paschal liturgy, such as the scripture readings and the eucharist. He says:

> Now the gloominess of the devilish winter has taken flight, and the joyousness of the heavenly meadow has flamed up; now the sadness of the dead has been run off, for the splendor of the resurrection has come. Let us all sing the new song, for the new and blessed song is fitting to the new citizenship. Let us sing the new song, for behold Adam has been renewed, for the ancient sin has been obliterated, "behold, all things have become new" (2 Cor. 5.17). Let us sing the new song from Miriam, the sister of Moses, for it is as fitting to us now as it was to them then. Let the chorus of those saints also be present to us and let it say what it sang then at the Red Sea, the "Let us sing to the Lord, for he has been magnified gloriously" (Ex. 15.4). For what has he done? "He has thrown horse and rider into the sea." Horse and rider: in the baptism of the bath he has drowned the horse, woman-crazy sin, on the one hand, and, on the other hand, the rider, the demon seated in sin. Therefore, "let us sing to the Lord for he has been magnified gloriously; for he has thrown Pharaoh and his force into the sea"; that is, he has purified with sea water the devil and the dark and accursed legion of his demons in the washing of baptism. I no longer fear to hear "You are dust and into dust you will depart" (Gen. 3.19); for in baptism I have laid aside the dust, and I have put on heaven, and I hear: "You are heaven and into the heavens you will depart"; "for as many of you as were baptized into Christ have put on Christ" (Gal. 3.27), and "as [was] the man of dust, so [are] those who are of dust, and as [is] the man of heaven, so [are] those who are of heaven" (1 Cor. 15.48). It is necessary for us to mount upon clouds and run back into the heavens; the word [is] not without witness; hear Paul saying "We will be caught up in clouds into a meeting with the Lord in the air and so we will be with the Lord always" (1 Thess. 4.17). Therefore, as we have just heard the psalmist exhorting and saying to us: "This is the day which the Lord has made, let us rejoice exceedingly and be glad in it" (Ps. 117.24). Therefore, let us not rejoice being stupefied by strong drink and intoxication, for this would not be merriment but folly and a moonless night of heart. Let us rejoice leaping in the spirit, let us rejoice feasting in love, being delighted in hope. But if it is necessary also to consider another merriment of heart, receiving with clean palms of hands the heavenly bread that is the travelling allowance of eternal life, let us swallow with the soul; but I mean receiving with clean palms, not washed by common water, but being made bright by beneficences. And let us draw for ourselves the divine and heavenly mixed wine with rosy lips, not blushing with crimson but being purplish with the blood of Jesus Christ.[65]

Christ's death is still a part of the mystery of the day, but Amphilochius continues to contrast the days of the Triemeron:

> O truly great and good day, in which the lamb is sacrificed and the world bought, and our shepherd lives: "For I am," he says, "the good shepherd" (Jn. 10.11). O new mystery and paradoxical wonder! A cross stood up, and Christ was spread over [it], and unjust death was what was visible, and a holy grave was what was coming to

be, a cross was what was visible and a bridal chamber was what was being fulfilled; yesterday a bridal chamber arose, and today a people has been begotten. O death of Christ, death of death and gushing forth with sweet life in the most bitter death. O mystery of Abraham being fulfilled in Christ! Isaac was bound hand and foot on the altar and a lamb was slain instead of him, and the son of God was raised upon a cross and was crucified in flesh in our behalf, and although the flesh was suffering, the divinity did not suffer. The sail of the cross stood in the ship of the world, and the sunless world waited; by this sail of the cross the one who sails does not know the shipwreck of death but sails up into heaven. Eve no longer fears the reproach of Adam, for in Mary her error has been restored; Adam no longer fears the serpent, for Christ has crushed the head of the dragon; "for you," it says, "have crushed the head of the dragon on the water" (Ps. 73.13); that is, at the time of baptism. I no longer lament, I no longer weep, saying "I have been tortured in distress in the thorn's having been stuck in me" (Ps. 31.4); for having come, Christ, having utterly destroyed the thorn of our sins, placed [it] upon his own head. My ancient condition has been destroyed, the old curse has been destroyed that says, "the earth will bring forth thorns and prickly plants for you" (Gen. 3.18); for the thorns have been dried up, the prickly plant has been uprooted, and the threefold crown has been placed upon my head. Who among Jews and Greeks believes that a tree stood and put forth life? And during each day it is gathered in my faithful ones and the fruit remains unexhausted; and every race and every people of faithful ones goes up on this tree to a seat of the soul and fills the bosom of the understanding with immortal fruit, and the tree lifts up all and feeds and seals and enriches all and after these things aims into heaven.[66]

The sources we have examined from Nyssa, Nazianzus, Caesarea, and Iconium show that, at least homiletically in this period, the breakdown of the Pascha into separate days with different themes had begun but was not yet complete and, in fact, appears to be progressing at different rates in the different areas.

But for how many days did they celebrate? The next section will address the question about whether or not Cappadocian Christians observed the Octave of Easter and the Great Fifty Days in the fourth century.

Disintegration of a Unitive Pentecost?

Interestingly, our earliest Cappadocian evidence of an extension of Pascha is attributed to Asterius Sophistes (d. c. 341), a Cappadocian Christian who apostasized during the persecution of Maximianus Herculius in the early fourth century, thereby forfeiting any chance at ordained ministry. According to Athanasius, Asterius was an early leader of Arian Christianity, who wrote a treatise (*Syntagmation*) at the request of the Eusebians[67] and then traveled around to the churches of Syria promoting his doctrine.[68] Socrates provides additional information:

> The bishops assembled at Constantinople deposed also Marcellus bishop of Ancyra, a city of Galatia Minor, on this account. A certain rhetorician of Cappadocia named Asterius having abandoned his art, and professed himself a convert to Christianity, undertook the composition of some treatises, which are still extant, in which he commended the dogmas of Arius; asserting that Christ is the power of God, in the same sense as the locust and the palmer-worm are said by Moses to be the power of God (Joel ii.25), with other similar utterances. Now Asterius was in constant association with the bishops, and especially with those of their number who did not discountenance the Arian doctrine: he also attended their Synods, in the hope of insinuating himself into the bishopric of some city: but he failed to obtain ordination, in consequence of having sacrificed during the persecution. Going therefore throughout the cities of Syria, he read in public the books which he had composed.[69]

There is no evidence that Asterius attended the Council of Nicea, but he apparently remained connected with his homeland, because he accompanied Bishop Dianius of Cappadocian Caesarea to the Synod of Antioch in 341. He probably died shortly thereafter.[70]

A collection of homilies on the Psalms was attributed to Asterius Sophistes in the seventeenth century by Louis Ellies du Pin and in later centuries by several other scholars, including Marcel Richard, who eventually published a critical edition of the texts of these homilies.[71] Among these homilies are several for the Easter Octave; if they were indeed composed by Asterius Sophistes,[72] they give us important information about paschal practices in Cappadocia during the period immediately before and after the Council of Nicea. For one thing, they show that there *was* an Easter Octave in Cappadocia (or wherever Asterius was preaching)[73] before 341. However, this raises a serious problem: why would a layperson who had lapsed in a persecution and accepted the teachings of Arius be allowed to compose (and deliver?) Easter Octave homilies? Perhaps the answer lies in his relationship with Dianius. Dianius baptized Basil in 357 and ordained him a reader in 360, but they had a falling out when Dianius subscribed to the Homoean creed put forth by the Council of Ariminum in 359.[74] Basil and Dianius were reconciled during the latter's last illness in 362, because he had been able to convince Basil that he had subscribed without understanding what he was doing and that he had never intended to renounce the teachings of Nicea.[75] It seems unlikely that Dianius, even if he was as simple as he claimed, would have included the Arian Asterius in his contingent to the Synod of Antioch so soon after the Council of Nicea, the teachings of which he clung to on his deathbed, according to Basil. It is more likely that Asterius's views had become more Nicene by the end of his life, as the Cappadocian and Arian church historian Philostorgius claims.[76] Richard, Auf der Maur and others adopt this position in order to be able to attribute the *Homilies on the Psalms*, which show no signs of Arianism, to Asterius.[77]

Most of the homilies are commentaries on Psalms 5, 8, 11, 14 and 18. Homily 11 on Psalm 5, for the Monday of the Octave, contains a section that, according to Cantalamessa, "may be seen as a preliminary to the *Exultet* [*sic*] and Easter preface."[78] Asterius says:

> It was a two-fold sight to see: while he was being crucified, the day was darkened, and while he was being raised, the night was illuminated like day. Why was the day darkened? Because it is written about him: "He has made darkness his hiding place" (Ps. 17.11). And why was the night illuminated like day? Because the prophet said to it: "Because darkness will not have been darkened with you, and night will have been illuminated like day" (Ps. 138.12). O night brighter than day; o night more beaming than the sun; o night whiter than snow; o night more brilliant than lightening; o night more radiant than lamps; o night more delightful than paradise; o night freed from darkness; o night filled with light; o night that drives away sleep; o night that teaches to be watchful with angels; o night that causes fear to the demons; o night [that is] desire of a year; o night [that is] marriage negotiator of the church; o night [that is] the mother of the neophytes; o night in which the devil, because he was dozing, has been stripped; o night in which the heir has led the heiress into the inheritance....[79]

This homily also describes some of the baptismal rites that these neophytes have recently undergone. Asterius addresses them:

> But you, o neophyte, after the Law, after the Prophets, after the Gospel, after teaching and catechesis, after the athlete's oil, after the bridal washing, after the spiritual anointing, after the bright garment, you have become a slave of the bondmaid, being enslaved to suffering. Flee the slavery of sin and receive the inheritance of adoption....[80]

Two other homilies reflect on other themes; one, for the Thursday of the Octave, describes the body of Christ (the church of neophytes and faithful) and its garment, and the other, for Friday, focuses entirely on the events of another Friday, the events around the crucifixion. The former includes an interesting spiritualization of the baptismal garment, comparing it to the robe of Aaron:

The queen, the church, has clothed herself in garments surpassing Aaron. In what way? Because the garment of Aaron, having been created in time, has been destroyed in time; but the garment of the church, being woven in one moment in the font, is the undecaying and uncorrupted woven robe of grace—for grace [is] with the ones who love the Lord Jesus Christ in incorruption (Eph. 6.24). Amen. The garment of Aaron was made from jacinth and fine linen and purple cloth and scarlet cloth (cf. Ex. 28.5ff); but the garment of the church has jacinth, the heavenly deity of Christ, and fine linen, the flesh from a virgin, and purple cloth, the passion—they wear the same purple (Mk. 15.17)—and scarlet cloth, the blood: "This is my blood" (Mk. 14.24). The garment of Aaron had tassels (shaped like pomegranates) (cf. Ex. 28.33–34) <...but the garment of the church has tassels>, the martyrs who pour out their blood for the sake of Christ, and their flowering brilliant words, the brilliant sponsors, and twelve bells, the apostles of Christ, who are ringing the message. For their voice rang out [into] all the earth (Ps. 18.5).[81]

Other than pointing to the existence of a paschal Octave, the most important thing about these homilies is, as Talley notes, that if there was a further extension of the paschal season to fifty days, there is no mention of it.[82] About forty years later Basil refers to such a season, but if such a unitive fifty-day season ever existed in Cappadocia, the writings of Basil's contemporaries indicate that it was already beginning to break down by this time. In *De Spiritu Sancto,* written to Amphilochius of Iconium around 375, Basil uses the term Πεντηκοστή to refer to the fifty-day season and does not link it specifically to the Holy Spirit. His concern is to illustrate his point that not all ecclesiastical customs derive from written scriptural mandates; some, such as standing for prayer on Sundays and during the Pentecost, derive from unwritten traditions. He writes:

Moreover all Pentecost is a reminder of the resurrection expected in the age to come. For that one and first day, if seven times multiplied by seven, completes the seven weeks of the holy Pentecost; for, beginning at the first, Pentecost ends with the same, making fifty revolutions through the like intervening days. And so it is a likeness of eternity, beginning as it does and ending, as this day the rules of the church have educated us to prefer the upright attitude of prayer, for by their plain reminder they, as it were, make our mind to dwell no longer in the present but in the future. Moreover every time we fall upon our knees and rise from off them we shew by the very deed that by our sin we fell down to earth, and by the loving kindness of our Creator were called back to heaven.[83]

However, in the literature under investigation, the term Πεντηκοστή more often refers to a single day, a day quite explicitly feasting the Holy Spirit. Just a few years after Basil wrote *De Spiritu Sancto,* Gregory of

Nazianzus says, "Honour the Day of the Spirit," and he appeals to the fact that we are now living in the "dispensation" of the Spirit.[84] He writes:

> We are keeping the feast of Pentecost and of the Coming of the Spirit, and the appointed time of the Promise, and the fulfillment of our hope. And how great, how august, is the Mystery. The dispensations of the Body of Christ are ended; or rather, what belongs to His Bodily Advent (for I hesitate to say the Dispensation of His Body, as long as no discourse persuades me that it is better to have put off the body), and that of the Spirit is beginning. And what were the things pertaining to the Christ? The Virgin, the Birth, the Manger, the Swaddling, the Angels glorifying Him, the Shepherds running to Him, the course of the Star, the Magi worshipping Him and bringing Gifts, Herod's murder of the children, the Flight of Jesus into Egypt, the Return from Egypt, the Circumcision, the Baptism, the Witness from Heaven, the Temptation, the Stoning for our sake (because He had to be given as an Example to us of enduring affliction for the Word), the Betrayal, the Nailing, the Burial, the Resurrection, the Ascension.... As to the things of the Spirit, may the Spirit be with me, and grant me speech as much as I desire; or if not that, yet as is in due proportion to the season. Anyhow He will be with me as my Lord; not in servile guise, nor awaiting a command, as some think. For He bloweth where He wills and on whom He wills, and to what extent He wills. Thus we are inspired both to think and to speak of the Spirit.[85]

A lengthy refutation of those who "reduce the Holy Spirit to the rank of a creature"[86] follows, and then to "our own friends,"[87] Gregory discourses about the progressive manifestation of the Spirit, "first in the heavenly and angelic powers," then in the patriarchs and prophets, then in Christ's disciples (pre-passion, post-resurrection and post-ascension) but not in Christ ("for I omit to mention Christ Himself, in Whom He dwelt, not as energizing, but as accompanying His Equal"). Of these three distinct manifestations to the disciples, Gregory writes, "Now the first of these manifests Him—the healing of the sick and casting out of evil spirits, which could not be apart from the Spirit; and so does that breathing upon them after the Resurrection, which was clearly a divine inspiration; and so too the *present distribution of the fiery tongues, which we are now commemorating.*"[88]

Almost a decade later, Gregory of Nyssa, preaching on the day of Pentecost, refers to it as the day "when the Pentecost is being completed" (τῆς Πεντηκοστῆς συμπληρουμένης).[89] For the most part, however, his homily *In Sanctem Pentecosten*[90] treats Pentecost as one day, feasting the Holy Spirit. The sermon opens with a glowing introductory praise of the psalter as a means of heightening the joy of the feast—David "emphasizes for us the splendor of the great feast of Pentecost, striking up the bow of the Spirit on the strings of wisdom" and "plays the part of this melody that corresponds to the grace of this moment: Come let us shout with joy to the Lord."[91] In the context of a commentary on a psalm, Gregory's main concern in this sermon is to defend his doctrine of the divinity of the Holy Spirit against the accusation being leveled by his opponents that he was introducing something new. First, he argues that divine revelation happens progressively.[92] Elie Moutsoulas summarizes the "well-ordered sequence" (ἀκολούθος τάξις) by which Gregory makes his argument:

> He recalls the state of man after the Fall, his separation from God and the love of God who progressively brought human life back to the knowledge of the Truth. First, we have the revelation by the prophets and the Law that there is only one God. Then, through the Gospel he revealed to us the Person of the only Son. Finally, the revelation of the Holy Spirit took place in the Church, 'in whom is life'. By the powerful breath of the Spirit, 'the spiritual forces of evil were scattered and the disciples who were in the upper room were filled with divine power'.[93]

After a brief discussion of the Pentecost event as described in Acts, Gregory takes a second approach to refuting his opponents, a pneumatological interpretation of Psalm 95. Gregory refers to Psalm 95:1—"Come, let us shout with joy to the Lord," a recurring refrain throughout the sermon—as an "ascription of praise to the Holy Spirit,"[94] having earlier interpreted it in the light of Paul's words in 2 Cor. 3.17: "But the Lord is the Spirit, just as the apostle says."[95] Then he cites Hebrews 3.7–9[96] to argue that the author ("the divine apostle") attributed God's words from Psalm 95.7–11 to the Holy Spirit.[97] Gregory then claims that Paul's attribution of the words of the psalm to the Holy Spirit clearly proves "that the Holy Spirit is God almighty"[98] and that "the mouths of the Pneumatomachoi who speak wickedness against God have been stopped...."[99] He concludes the sermon with a series of wishes for his opponents—that they will receive the sweet wine they accuse him of being filled with, that they will be filled with the new wine that has not been spoiled by being mixed with "the water of heresy," that they will be completely filled with the Holy Spirit.[100] He thinks his opponents incapable of these things but exhorts his listeners, "let us be delighted in the gift of the Holy Spirit and let us exult in this day that the Lord has made in Christ."[101]

Significantly, both of these Pentecost sermons use the occasion of the feast of the Holy Spirit to reinforce belief in the divinity of the Holy Spirit and to refute those who denied that belief. This is not surprising, given that the two Gregorys—along with Basil and Amphilochius—were deeply involved in the pneumatological controversies that led to and continued after the Council of Constantinople in 381. Were the struggles with the Pneumatomachians and others directly *responsible* for the dismemberment of an earlier multi-themed fiftieth day after Pascha and a contributing factor to the breakdown of what Basil knew as a fifty-day season? If so, this would presuppose an intermediate step—that the fiftieth day already carried more festal weight than the forty-eight days between it and Easter. Is there evidence of such a step? In order to try to answer these questions, it is necessary to examine another new feature of the Cappadocian calendar: what conclusions can be drawn from the fact that in Cappadocia in the last quarter of the fourth century, as in a few other places in this period, Christians began to commemorate Christ's ascension on the *fortieth* day after Pascha?

Ascension

Daniélou thinks that the Pneumatomachian issue was instrumental in the Cappadocian dismantling of a fiftieth day that by this time was about both the ascension of Christ and the descent of the Holy Spirit. In fact, he maintains that Gregory of Nyssa's sermon for the Feast of the Ascension is *the* earliest evidence we possess of such an observance on the fortieth day. He also suggests that it is highly likely that Gregory was the mastermind behind the separation of the two commemorations and that he did so in order to devote the fiftieth day exclusively to the descent of the Holy Spirit (whose consubstantiality with the Father had recently been affirmed by the Council of Constantinople) and to refute the Pneumatomachians and others who denied the Holy Spirit's divinity. [102]

Our discussion in this section will address several questions. Is Gregory of Nyssa's *In Ascensionem Christi*,[103] which is among the earliest evidence we possess of a commemoration of Christ's ascension on a day other than the fiftieth day of the paschal season, *the* earliest? Can we identify Gregory as the originator of the separate Feast of the Ascension on the fortieth day? What was "the day called ἐπισῳζομένη" referred to in the title of the sermon? Is there any evidence that Christ's ascension was *ever* commemorated on the fiftieth day in Cappadocia?

Let us try to answer this last question first. There is sparse evidence that Christ's ascension was among the events celebrated on the fiftieth day after Easter in some places. The Syriac document known as the *Doctrina Apos-*

tolorum, which according to F.C. Burkitt reflects the practices of fourth- or possibly third-century Edessa, refers to such a commemoration on the fiftieth day. *De solemnitate paschali*, written by Eusebius of Caesarea in Palestine around 332, contains the first known use of ἀνάληψις to refer to a *feast*, and this feast is held on the fiftieth day.[104] From Egeria, we know that the commemoration of Christ's ascension was still a part of the activities of the fiftieth day for the Jerusalem community when she visited in 383, although it was commemorated separately from the celebration of the descent of the Holy Spirit.[105]

So there is evidence that a festal observance of the ascension took place on the fiftieth day after Easter in some areas of Syria and Palestine in the fourth century, but was that also the case in Cappadocia? Daniélou, appealing to a sermon for Mid-Pentecost (Μεσοπεντηκόστη) that is sometimes attributed to Amphilochius, accepts its Amphilochian authenticity and interprets it as evidence that in the time of Amphilochius, the ascension was being commemorated as part of the Day of Pentecost, at least in nearby Iconium. He writes, "But the context indeed appears to show that it alludes to the celebration of the mystery of the Ascension on the fiftieth day, since it emphasizes that the Μεσοπεντηκόστη is situated in the middle of the two great feasts of Easter and Ascension."[106] However, Daniélou misreads the text and draws too definite a conclusion from very vague information. The sermon actually states that the "present middle feast" lies between "the resurrection and the *Pentecost*," and "it made known the resurrection, points to the Pentecost, trumpets the ascension."[107] It is hard to know how to interpret the fact that the trumpeting of the ascension follows the pointing out of the Pentecost in the text and to determine precisely when the ascension was observed. However, it is clear that the second feast mentioned is Pentecost, not Ascension, as Daniélou claims, and to conclude from this vague evidence that Cappadocian Christians celebrated the ascension on the fiftieth day after Easter seems hasty. In any case, the homily cannot be confidently used as evidence of fourth-century Cappadocian practice. While Cabié also accepts it as the authentic work of Amphilochius and treats it as the earliest evidence of the Mid-Pentecost feast,[108] Cornelis Datema has shown, based on manuscript and internal evidence, that it is probably not authentic and was likely composed in the late sixth century.[109]

Without this Mid-Pentecost sermon, there is no evidence that a commemoration of Christ's ascension was *ever* a part of the Cappadocian Christians' celebration of the fiftieth day. This is not to say that it was not; however, to say that it was is to reconstruct Cappadocian practice on the basis of information—and sparse information at that—from other regions. So while there is evidence that a festal observance of the ascension took place on the fiftieth day after Easter in some areas of Syria and Palestine, there is no specific indication that this was the case in Cappadocia, unless we accept Cabié's postulation that Constantinople and its environs followed Palestinian practice in this matter.[110]

Since we cannot establish with certainty that there was an ascension element in the Cappadocian fiftieth day, we cannot be sure that Gregory of Nyssa relocated such an element from the fiftieth to the fortieth day. Yet could he have been the originator of the Feast of the Ascension on the fortieth day, either by creating something completely new or by moving something from another day? It is possible. Daniélou claims that Gregory's ascension sermon is the earliest evidence we have of such a feast.[111] However, even if Gregory's sermon is the earliest evidence we have, indications of celebrations of the ascension on the fortieth day after Easter start lurking about the sources from other areas only slightly later. John Chrysostom's *De Sacra Pentecoste* I, delivered during his time in Antioch (386–398), *De Sacra Pentecoste* II, and the existence of his sermon *In Ascensione* indicate that this feast was observed separately from Pentecost in Antioch. Another Syrian source, the Church Order known as the *Apostolic Constitutions*, is sometimes considered to contain the earliest clear evidence of a celebration of the Feast of the Ascension on the fortieth day. This document is generally dated between 375 and 380 , which would indeed make it our earliest witness. Chromatius, bishop of Aquileia from 388 to 407, also knew of and preached on the Feast of the Ascension forty days after Easter in his *De ascensione domini*.[112] Filastrius of Brescia's *Diversarum haereseon liber* mentions a feast celebrating the ascension "near Pentecost" and later places it specifically on the fortieth day after Easter.[113] Of these sources from East and West, Talley points out, "If all these are, as Daniélou argues, later than Gregory of Nyssa's sermon of 388, they would seem to be so slightly later that the difference in time would not be of great significance for the history of the festival."[114]

The meaning of the term ἐπισωζομένη is still unclear; in one of Chrysostom's homilies and in the *Apostolic Constitutions* it is used to refer to the Sunday before the fortieth day but with no allusion to the Ascension.[115]

Daniélou thinks that in Gregory's text it is the previous designation, "the traditional name of the day," to which the reference to the Ascension has been added by Gregory. [116] Unfortunately, without additional information about the referent of this term, its appearance in Gregory's title does not shed much light on the question.

Pentecost Conclusions

The paschal season was undergoing significant shifts during the period in Cappadocia, as it was elsewhere. There is some evidence of the existence of an Octave after Pascha and of a fifty-day season of paschal rejoicing. We have also seen that by the time of the two Gregorys, the fiftieth day after Pascha did indeed carry more festal weight than the other forty-eight days between the two feasts, because it had clearly become the Feast of the Holy Spirit. We have also seen, however, that there is no evidence that commemoration of Christ's ascension was ever part of the festal agenda of this day in Cappadocia, although this was the case in other areas. The first evidence we have of such a commemoration is Gregory of Nyssa's sermon, which places it on the fortieth day after Pascha, around the same time that the same development appears in the sources from Antioch and Northern Italy. The last section of this chapter will address the question of how much the doctrinal controversies of the day influenced these shifts.

First, however, we must explore the *pre*-paschal season, the pattern and meaning of Lent in fourth-century Cappadocia.

The Shape of Lent

Talley observes that "...the Council of Nicea is something of a watershed for the fast of forty days. Prior to Nicea, no record exists of such a forty-day fast before Easter. Only a few years after the council, however, we encounter it in most of the Church as either a well-established custom or one that has become so nearly universal as to impinge on those churches that have not yet adopted it."[117] Just which forty days they were—or whether the actual number of fasting days even *was* forty—were matters of local variation. Our task in this section is to ascertain, if possible, where Cappadocia fell along the fourth-century spectrum of Lenten patterns and interpretations.

Before examining the Cappadocian sources, let us establish that spectrum for purposes of comparison. Our earliest clear evidence of a forty-day prepaschal fast is found in the second Festal Letter of Athanasius of Alexandria, which was written in 330. From this letter and Athanasius's other Festal Letters, we know that Lent in Alexandria in the years just after the Council of Nicea was six weeks long, including the six days of the Paschal Fast immediately preceding Easter. Sundays and Sabbaths (except the day before Easter) were not fasted. We also note that Athanasius viewed Lent as a time of fasting in preparation for the Pascha; these letters contain no mention of baptismal preparation or imitation of Jesus' fast in the wilderness.[118]

To his Festal Letter of 340, which is no longer extant, Athanasius appended a cover letter, which has survived, to his friend Serapion, Bishop of Thmuis. In it, he wrote: "But O, my beloved, whether in this way or any other, persuade and teach them to fast the forty days. For it is a disgrace that when all the world does this, those alone who are in Egypt, instead of fasting, should find their pleasure."[119] Athanasius wrote this letter from exile in Rome, so apparently the Lenten fast was being observed there in 340, if not by "all the world" as Athanasius claims. However, in Rome the actual number of fasting days was thirty-six; the season was six weeks long as in Alexandria, but Sabbaths were fasted. Also as in Alexandria, the Paschal Fast was included in the Lenten Fast.[120]

By the time of Ambrose's episcopate (374–397), Christians in Milan also observed a six-week Lent, the last week of which was Holy Week, but they did not fast Sabbaths. The purpose of Lent in Milan was preparation for baptism and reconciliation of penitents.[121]

The *Apostolic Constitutions* also indicates a six-week pre-paschal fast for fourth-century Christians in Syria. However, at the conclusion of the Lenten fast, this document directs that fasting is to cease for two days and then the six-day Paschal Fast is to begin.[122] Talley notes, "This is the pattern of fourth-century Antioch and will be the pattern of the prepaschal fasts at Constantinople, at Jerusalem in the fifth century, at Alexandria in the seventh, and eventually throughout the oriental churches. In this system, Lent and Holy Week are totally distinct."[123]

Egeria informs us that in Jerusalem at this time Lent consisted of seven weeks of five fast days each plus one week (Great Week) in which Saturday was also fasted, making a total of forty-one fast days.[124]

Information about fourth-century Constantinopolitan practice is limited. However, according to the church historian Sozomen, who lived and wrote in

Constantinople in the early fifth century, Lent in the imperial city and its "neighboring provinces as far as Phoenicia" was seven weeks long.[125]

What pattern did Cappadocian Christians follow, and how did they interpret Lent? In his *Oration 40 On Holy Baptism*, preached the day after Epiphany in either 380 or 381,[126] Gregory of Nazianzus indicates that Lent was forty days long. Apparently, some were resisting his exhortations to be baptized as soon as possible on the grounds that Jesus waited until he was thirty years old. One of Gregory's responses to this situation is that Jesus gave us patterns to follow, but not necessarily to emulate exactly. In explaining, he also gives us information about Lent:

> For there are many other details of the Gospel History which are quite different to what happens nowadays, and the seasons of which do not correspond. For instance Christ fasted a little before His temptation, we before Easter. As far as the fasting days are concerned it is the same, but the difference in the season is no little one. He armed Himself with them against temptation; but to us this fast is symbolical of dying with Christ, and it is a purification in preparation for the festival. And He fasted absolutely for forty days, for He was God; but we measure our fasting by our power, even though some are led by zeal to rush beyond their strength.[127]

In his first homily on the Forty Martyrs of Sebaste, Gregory of Nyssa also indicates that Lent was forty days long. He says, "This was the time; these [are] the days of the struggle; this is the opening of the Pascha, the mystery of the holy period of forty days. The forty days of propitiation to you and the crowns of the struggles are equal in number."[128]

Asterius of Amaseia provides a few more clues. He calls Lent "the Holy Forty" (ἡ ἁγία Τεσσαρακοστή) in his homily on the beginning of the "holy fasts." He says, "Therefore, all you pupils of philosophy and lovers of the high things and disciples of the word, love the present time and the Holy Forty, rejoicing to welcome [it] as a teacher of self-control and a mother of virtue and a nurse of the sons of God and a guide of the undisciplined and a calm of souls and a tranquility of life and a gently disposed and unconfused peace."[129]

Unfortunately, this sermon does not contain specifics about how those forty days were arranged. However, a much earlier sermon, Basil's *In ebriosos*, which Bernardi claims was delivered on Easter of 372,[130] does provide a clue. In this homily, Basil refers to "these seven consecutive weeks of the fast."[131] This information suggests that Cappadocia's Lent was similar in pattern to what Sozomon observed in Constantinople early in the following century.

Basil's two homilies concerning fasting, which Bernardi dates to the Sunday immediately preceding Lent 371,[132] provide some additional clues about how Lent was arranged. Unfortunately, they do not contain further information about the duration of Lent in Caesarea in this period; however, they do suggest that the people fasted (or were supposed to fast!) for five days each week. In urging his listeners to let the household rest by fasting and, therefore, not requiring food preparation, Basil says, "Let the fast become rest from continuous works.... Let the belly also give some vacation to the mouth, let it make a peace treaty of five days with you, it who always demands and never abates, who takes today and forgets tomorrow."[133] Later he exhorts:

> Do not let strong drink initiate you to a fast. Entrance into a fast is not through strong drink; for neither into righteousness through greediness nor into soundness of mind through licentiousness, nor, to say in sum, into goodness through evil. The door to a fast is different. Strong drink leads into licentiousness, self-sufficiency to a fast. The one who contends is trained beforehand; the one who fasts is self-controlled beforehand. Not as one who defends yourself against the days, not as one who outwits the lawgiver, throw out the drunken headache before the five days.[134]

In De jejunio II, Basil says, "Therefore, make yourself worthy of the holy fast; do not ruin tomorrow's self-control with today's strong drink. The reasoning is bad, the notion is evil; 'since a fast of five days is publicly proclaimed to us, today let us drown ourselves with strong drink.'"[135] And again: "But on the other hand, I fear strong drink, which the winelovers save just like some paternal share. For as those who depart for long journeys, so some of the foolish buy wine today for the five days of the fasts."[136]

If Bernardi's assessment of the nine sermons of Basil's Hexaemeron is correct, this homiletical collection on Creation provides additional evidence that the Christians of Cappadocia fasted for five days in each of the weeks of Lent. Bernardi notes that these sermons were preached over five consecutive days and that the eighth at least was delivered on a fast day. For Bernardi, this information suggests the eastern Lenten pattern of fasting five days each week. He concludes that Basil preached Homilies I–IV (one sermon each morning and one each evening) on Monday and Tuesday of a week in Lent 378, Homilies VI–IX on the Thursday and Friday, and Homily V on Wednesday. He offers two possible explanations for the fact that there is only one homily for Wednesday; either someone else preached at the other gathering, or Basil preached on some other topic, possibly a catechetical sermon.[137]

Concerning the practice of gathering the faithful for a sermon both morning and evening during Lent, Bernardi also cites a passage from *De jejunio* II, in which Basil says, "Therefore, the Holy Spirit will feast you all the days consecutively, in the mornings and also in the evening festivities. Let no one be voluntarily absent from the spiritual banquet."[138] By "spiritual banquet" (πνευματικὴ εὐωχία), Basil means "sermon," according to Bernardi;[139] if his assessment is correct, this gives us another glimpse into Cappadocian practice.

Apparently, as seems to have been the case in Basil's Caesarea twenty-five years earlier, Asterius's community in Amaseia did not fast Sabbaths. At one point he exhorts his listeners, "Do not become sad like a child being dragged off to school, do not murmur against the days of purity, do not seek the end of the week as the coming of spring after a bitter winter, do not long for the Sabbath for the sake of drunkenness like a Jew, do not count the days of the Forty like a lazy servant awaiting the end of the appointed time of hire...."[140]

So while the evidence is scant, the few scraps we do have suggest that, for most of our period, Christians in this area—at least the important sees of Caesarea and Amaseia—followed the pattern of not fasting Sabbaths and Sundays, as was the case in Jerusalem and Antioch at this time.

Asterius's *interpretation* of the Lenten fast is somewhat unexpected, especially if we come to the data hoping to find it dripping with paschal and baptismal imagery. This sermon is entirely about the benefits of fasting to both body and soul; there is no mention of fasting in preparation for Pascha or baptism. "Fasting is an intimate friend of the saints; fasting is originator of every good deed," and it is the tool without which the righteous characters and workers of wonders in the Hebrew scriptures could not have succeeded.[141] Asterius recommends that Christians fast for six months out of every year, giving equal time to body and soul,[142] although he himself can only manage two months.[143] Apparently some were resisting the fast, claiming that it caused sickness; Asterius disagrees, saying that, on the contrary, fasting produces health![144] Another benefit of fasting is that it prefigures the Christian eschatological hope; "A self-controlled life is an image of the future and incorruptible life."[145]

Despite Bernardi's suggestion that the "missing" sermon of Basil's *Hex-*

aemeron may have been a catechetical one because Lent was the period of baptismal preparation,[146] Basil's sermons likewise do not focus on baptism. In fact, his concerns are remarkably similar to those Asterius would address two decades later. First, Basil distances Christian fasting from that of the Jews. He begins *De jejunio* I by quoting Psalm 80.4:

> 'Sound the trumpets at the new moon,' it says, 'in the glorious day of your feast.' This command is prophetic. But more loudly than any trumpet and more clearly than any musical instrument, the readings signal to us the advancing feast of the days. For we have made known the grace of the fasts from Isaiah (Is. 58.4, 6), on the one hand having rejected the Jewish manner of the fast, but on the other hand having represented to us the true fast. Do not fast into judgments and battles, but loose every bond of injustice. And the Lord [says]: 'Do not be sullen, but wash your face, and anoint your head (Mt. 16.17).' Let us be disposed, therefore, as we have been taught, not looking gloomy in the approaching days, but beamingly to them, as it is clearly suitable for saints....[147]

According to Basil, the Christian fast is not only a *truer* fast, but it is also *older*; he asks, "Do you suppose that I reckon its origin from the law? The fast is even older than the law."[148] He explains that the fast originated in Paradise, because God instructed Adam and Eve not to eat of the Tree of the Knowledge of Good and Evil, but wine-drinking is a more recent development, having come into being after the Flood.[149] For Asterius, fasting prefigures the Reign of God; Basil expresses a similar notion, although for him the fast seems to be more a means to that end than an image of that end. He says, "Since we did not fast, we fell from paradise; therefore, let us fast, in order that we might return to it."[150] Like Asterius, Basil discusses some figures of the Hebrew Scriptures, who succeeded in their various careers only when they were faithful practitioners of the fast, or who were unsuccessful because they chose to satisfy the belly rather than obey God. After citing the examples of Moses, Esau, Samuel's mother, Anna, and Samson, Basil concludes:

> A fast begets prophets, it strengthens strong ones; a fast instructs lawgivers, good protection of soul; steadfast fellow-inhabitant with body; tool to those who are bravest; exercise to athletes. This beats off trials; this stimulates to piety, fellow inhabitant of soberness, maker of self-control. It behaves bravely in battles, it teaches solitude in peace. It consecrates the Nazirite, it completes the priest. For it is not possible to behave boldly toward worship without a fast; not only now in the mystical and true worship, but also in the type that is being offered according to the law.[151]

After illustrating this point with a few more examples from the Hebrew scriptures, Basil concludes his sermon by expanding the parameters of the fast, telling his listeners that the true fast is not only from foods but also from injustice, judgment, battles, wanton acts, and litigation.[152]

In *De jejunio* II, Basil promotes the fast by contrasting soldiers and athletes who contend against spiritual enemies—his listeners, ideally—with those whose enemies are merely earthly. He says:

> And, therefore, the word of exhortation is absolutely necessary to me, both as I appoint the soldiers of Christ to the battle against the invisible enemies and prepare the athletes of piety for crowns of righteousness through self-control. What, then, do I say, brothers? That, on the one hand, it is suitable for those who attend to battle tactics and those who are exercised in wrestling schools to make themselves plump with abundance of food, so that they may take part more vigorously in the exercises; but, on the other hand, to whom "the battle is not against blood and flesh, but against the rulers and the powers and the world-rulers of this darkness, against the spiritual things of evil," [Eph. 6.12] to these it is necessary to be disciplined for the contest through self- control and fast. For olive oil fattens the athlete, but a fast strengthens the athlete of piety. For this reason, as you gradually diminish the flesh, as much will you cause the soul to be bright with spiritual vigor.[153]

He continues the metaphor by discussing the differences between the equipment of soldiers of the world and that of spiritual soldiers, saying:

> ...[T]hus it is clear that the same foods do not produce strength in both; but, on the one hand, the lessons of piety strengthen us, but, on the other hand, to them the satiety of the belly is a necessity. Therefore, since the current time has brought to us these much-anticipated days, let us all gladly welcome [them] as ancient nurses through whom the Church has nursed us to piety. Therefore, being about to fast, do not look sullen in the Jewish manner, but adorn yourself with the Gospel, not bewailing the need of the belly, but rejoicing together with the soul for the spiritual enjoyment.[154]

Basil warns the faithful not to show up the next day with alcohol on their breath; he says, "The Lord admits the one who fasts within the holy precincts; he does not accept the one who has a sick headache, as [s/he is] profane and unholy. For if you come tomorrow smelling of wine, and this rotten, how will I reckon your drunken headache into the fast? ...How will I assign you? Among the drunks or among the fasters?"[155] Then he explains how fasting benefits all sorts of creatures—as well as society at large:

A fast guards young animals, corrects the young person, makes the old man revered; for old age governed by fast [is] more venerable.... It corrects every city as a whole and every country to good order, it calms clamor, it banishes strife, it silences abuse.... Gentle laughs and harlots' warps [of looms] and mad dances suddenly go quietly out of the city, just as those who have been banished by some hard judge, the fast. But if everyone undertook it as the advisor in behalf of the things to be done, nothing would prevent there being deep peace throughout the whole inhabited world; neither nations rising up against each other nor armies meeting in battle. Tools would not be forged when a fast held sway, neither would courts be organized, nor would any inhabit the prisons; nor would the deserts everywhere have those who do evil, nor the cities swindlers, nor the sea pirates. If all were disciples of the fast, the voice of the tax collector would not have been heard, according to the word of Job, nor would our life be full of groaning and infected by gloominess, if a fast regulated our life. For it is clear that it would have taught everyone self-control not only from foods, but also from avarice and from greediness and [it would have taught] complete flight and estrangement from every evil.[156]

As in *De jejunio* I, Basil expands the notion of fasting by applying it to more than just food and strong drink:

Therefore, if you wish to return to God through the confession, flee from strong drink, do not make for yourself the more painful estrangement. Although abstinence from foods does not by itself suffice for the praiseworthy fast, let us fast an acceptable fast, pleasing to God. A true fast, the estrangement of evil, self-control of tongues, cessation of passions, separation from desires, from evil speech, from falsehood, from false oath. The lack of these things is a true fast. Therefore, the good fast [is] in these things.[157]

A warning concludes the sermon:

Do not let the fast that was threatened to the Jews come also upon us; "For behold the days are coming," says the Lord, "and I will bring this famine upon the earth, not a famine of bread, nor thirst for water, but a famine of hearing the word of the Lord" (Amos 8.11); which for this reason the righteous judge brought on, when he saw our mind, on the one hand, being weakened in the atrophy of the lessons of the truth, but our outer man, on the other hand, being made exceedingly fat and fleshy.[158]

The data about Lent in fourth-century Cappadocia are scant; however, our examination of the sources that do exist suggest that by the last quarter of the century, it was described as a forty-day period but was actually a seven-week period during which five days were fasted each week. We know from the Easter homilies discussed above that Cappadocian Christians practiced paschal baptism in this period, but despite the fact that those homilies are drenched (or at least damp) with baptismal imagery and information, the Lenten homilies that we possess make no reference to baptismal preparation, with the exception of Asterius Sophistes' brief mention of pre-baptismal catechesis.[159] The rest of the sermons focus instead on the physical and spiritual benefits of the ascetic discipline of fasting. Gregory of Nazianzus does situate Lent in relation to Easter; in the passage cited above, he writes, "He armed Himself with them [fasting days] against temptation; but to us this fast is symbolical of dying with Christ, and it is a purification in preparation for the festival." However, he does not provide details about what that preparation entailed.

Doctrinal Issues and Paschal Developments

There is very little polemical material in the Easter and Lenten sermons we have discussed. Gregory of Nazianzus warns his congregation not to follow strangers who would "lead you away from the sound Faith in the Father, the Son, and the Holy Ghost, the One Power and Godhead...."[160] As might be expected, there is some anti-Jewish rhetoric, usually accompanied by criticism of the Greeks.[161] In one place, Gregory of Nazianzus does turn on the Arians in the context of his Easter discussion of the incarnation, using the exact same words he used in his Christmas sermon.[162]

Talley notes that in Chromatius's Ascension sermon "the feast is commended with a zeal that could suggest it is of recent appearance."[163] It is interesting to note that in Gregory of Nyssa's Ascension sermon, there is none of this "hard sell" that one might expect from a bishop trying to institute something new in the life of his congregation nor is there a whisper of the polemics one might expect at an occasion newly created as a result of an anti-heresy agenda.

However, as discussed above,[164] the Pentecost sermons of the two Gregorys, preached just before and just after the Council of Constantinople, are full of refutation of Pneumatomachian teaching. Whether or not Pentecost's thematic shift was a conscious strategy in the pneumatological struggles, once the day *did* become the feast of the Spirit, it was a natural opportunity for our preachers to communicate their ideas about right pneumatology.

Notes

1. Because these Christians observed Pascha on 14 Nisan, they were labeled Quarto-decimans, "Fourteenthers."
2. *Epistula Apostolorum* 15.
3. Talley, *Origins* 6.
4. Ibid., 7–8.
5. Ibid., 8–9; Bradshaw, *Search*, 195.
6. For Sardis, Melito, *Peri Pascha*, composed c. 160–170; for Ephesus, Eusebius Pamphili, *Historia Ecclesiastic* 5.24 preserves a letter from Polycrates, bishop of Ephesus c. 190, to Victor, bishop of Rome, which indicates that Ephesus was Quartodeciman; Polycrates's letter claims that John, Philip, Polycarp of Smyrna, Thrasea of Eumenia, Sagaris of Laodicea, Papirius, Melito of Sardis and Polycrates's seven predecessors at Ephesus were all Quartodecimans; also for Laodicea, Anatolius, *Canons about the Pascha*; for Hieropolis, Apollinarius, *On the Pascha*, c. 166.
7. Eusebius Pamphili, *Ecclesiastical History*, trans. Roy J. Deferrari, *The Fathers of the Church: A New Translation*, vol. 19, ed. Roy Joseph Deferrari *et al.*, (New York: Fathers of the Church, Inc., 1953), 5.23, 333–334; subsequent references to this English translation of Eusebius will be cited as *FOTC* by book, section and page numbers.
8. Firmilian to Cyprian, Letter 74.6, *The Ante-Nicene Fathers: Translations of the Writings of the Fathers Down to A.D. 325*, ed. Alexander Roberts and James Donaldson (New York: Charles Scribner's Sons, 1926), vol. 5, *Hippolytus, Cyprian, Caius, Novatian, Appendix*, 391; subsequent references from this series will be cited as *ANF*.
9. Anscar J. Chupungco, OSB, *Shaping the Easter Feast*, NPM Studies in Church Music and Liturgy (Washington, D.C.: The Pastoral Press, 1992), 44.
10. Ibid., 46.
11. Constantine, *Letter to the Churches* 18, Raniero Cantalamessa, *Easter in the Early Church: An Anthology of Jewish and Early Christian Texts*, rev. ed., trans. James M. Quigley, SJ and Joseph T. Lienhard, SJ (Collegeville, Minn.: The Liturgical Press, 1993), 63; subsequent references to this volume will be cited as Cantalamessa.
12. The concern for uniformity in this matter was a relatively new development, perhaps another reflection of Constantine's desire to unify the Christians of his empire. In an earlier controversy over Quartodeciman practice, Irenaeus of Lyons rebuked Victor of Rome for attempting to excommunicate those who observed Pascha on Passover, citing an even earlier disagreement in which Anicetus of Rome and Polycarp agreed to disagree, apparently unruffled by the divergence of practice (Eusebius Pamphili, *Historia Ecclesiastica*, 5.24).
13. Chupungco, 47–8.
14. Ibid., 93.
15. Eusebius, *Vita Constantini* III.19.
16. Epiphanius of Salamis, *Panarion haereseon*, 50.1,3–8, *The Panarion of Epiphanius of Salamis: Books II and III (Sects 47–80, De Fide)*, trans. Frank Williams, Nag Hammadi and Manichaean Studies 36, ed. J.M. Robinson and H.J. Klimkeit (Leiden: E.J. Brill, 1994), 23–24. I would like to thank the Reverend Dr. Thomas Talley

for bringing this passage to my attention.

17. See Alan E. Samuel, *Greek and Roman Chronology: Calendars and Years in Classical Antiquity* (Munich: C.H. Beck'sche Verlagsbuchhandlung, 1972), 177. The Cappadocian calendar consisted of twelve thirty-day months plus five epagomenal days inserted between the eleventh and twelfth months.

18. Gregory of Nyssa, "On the Three-Day Period of the Resurrection of our Lord Jesus Christ (De Tridui Spatio)", trans. S.G. Hall, *The Easter Sermons of Gregory of Nyssa: Translation and Commentary*, eds. Andreas Spira and Christoph Klock, Patristic Monograph Series 9 (Cambridge, Mass.: The Philadelphia Patristic Foundation, 1981), 43–44. Subsequent references to this volume will be cited as *ESGN*.

19. Cantalamessa maintains that "This oration was pronounced during an Easter vigil in Gregory's later years (386–395)" (Cantalamessa, 174). Because of some of the phrases used in this sermon, Bernardi maintains that it was not preached to Gregory's own congregation at Nyssa; he suggests that it may have been delivered at Constantinople, Caesarea or Sebaste. Bernardi does not address Gregory's discussion about the fourteenth (Bernardi, 287).

20. Chupungco, 74.

21. Gregory of Nyssa, "On the Three-Day Period of the Resurrection of our Lord Jesus Christ," *ESGN*, 44.

22. Ibid., 45–46.

23. Meredith, "The Answer to Jewish Objections (De Tridui Spatio p. 294.14–298.18)," in *ESGN*, 294.

24. Gregory of Nyssa, Letter 1, *NPNF*, Series 2, vol. 5, 527.

25. Jean Daniélou, "La Chronologie des Sermons de Grégoire de Nysse," *Revue des sciences religieuses* 29 (1955), 372; hereafter cited as "Chronologie."

26. Gregory of Nyssa, "Discourse on the Holy Pascha," *ESGN*, 6–7.

27. Ibid., 8–9.

28. Gregory of Nyssa, "In luciferam sanctam Domini resurrectionem," *GNO* 9.1, 318.20–21.

29. Gregory of Nyssa, "On the Three-Day Period of the Resurrection of our Lord Jesus Christ," *ESGN*, 31.

30. Ibid., 4–6. The scripture reference is Gen. 26.4.

31. Ibid., 31–32.

32. Ibid., 32. Scripture references are Gen. 22 and Ex. 17.8–16.

33. Ibid., 32–33. Scripture references are Is. 7.14; 53.7 and Jonah 2.1.

34. Ibid., 35.

35. Ibid.

36. Ibid., 36.

37. Ibid., 37.

38. Ibid., 37–38.

39. Ibid., 39–41.

40. Thomas K. Carroll and Thomas Halton, eds., *Liturgical Practice in the Fathers*, Message of the Fathers of the Church, no. 21 (Wilmington, D. E.: Michael Glazier, 1988), 236. Subsequent references to texts in this volume will be cited as Carroll and Halton.

41. According to Daniélou, this sermon was delivered on April 9, 388 (Daniélou,

"Chronologie," 372).

42. Gregory of Nyssa, "The Holy and Saving Pascha," *ESGN*, 51.

43. Cantalamessa, 14.

44. Dom Gregory Dix, *The Shape of the Liturgy*, 2d ed. (Westminster, England: Dacre Press, 1945; reprint, 1954), 333ff.

45. Gregory of Nazianzus, *Oration 1 On Easter and His Reluctance*, 1–2, *NPNF*, vol. 7, 203.

46. Ibid., 3–4, Cantalamessa, 75–76.

47. Cantalamessa, 172–3, n. c.

48. Ibid.

49. Wolfgang Huber, *Passa und Ostern: Untersuchungen zur Osterfeier der alten Kirche*, Beihefte zur Zeitschrift für die neutestamentliche Wissenschaft 35 (Berlin: Töpelmann, 1969), 194–195.

50. Gregory of Nazianzus, *Oration 45 The Second Oration on Easter* 2, *NPNF*, Series 2, vol. 7, 423.

51. Ibid., 4, *NPNF*, 424.

52. Ibid., 21, *NPNF*, 431.

53. Ibid., 24–25.

54. Gregory of Nazianzus, Letter 120.

55. Basil of Caesarea, *Exhortatoria ad sanctum baptisma* 1.

56. This sermon was delivered some time during Amphilochius's episcopate but cannot be more precisely dated (Cantalamessa, 174).

57. Paul F. Bradshaw, "The Origins of Easter," in *Passover and Easter: Origin and History to Modern Times*, Two Liturgical Traditions, ed. Paul F. Bradshaw and Lawrence A. Hoffman, no. 5 (Notre Dame, Ind.: University of Notre Dame Press, 1999), 95, n. 22.

58. Amphilochius of Iconium, Oration 5 *In diem Sabbati Sancti* 1.

59. Ibid.1.

60. Ibid. 3.

61. Ibid. 4.

62. The Greek title is Τοῦ μακαρίου Ἀμφιλοχίου ἐπισκόπου Ἰκονίου περὶ τῶν νεοφωτίστων καὶ εἰς τὴν ἀνάστασιν τοῦ σωτῆρος ἡμῶν Ἰησοῦ Χριστοῦ, "Of the blessed Amphilochius Bishop of Iconium concerning the neophytes and on the resurrection of our Savior Jesus Christ."

63. Amphilochius of Iconium, Oration 7 *De recens baptizatis* 1.

64. Ibid. 2.

65. Ibid. 3.

66. Ibid. 4.

67. The Eusebians were followers of Eusebius, Arian bishop of Nicomedia (d. c. 342), who was a fellow-student with Arius of Lucian of Antioch.

68. Athanasius of Alexandria, *De synodis* 18.2.

69. Socrates, *The Ecclesiastical History by Socrates Scholasticus*, 1.36, *NPNF*, Series 2, vol. 2, 33.

70. Wolfram Kinzig, *In Search of Asterius: Studies on the Authorship of the Homilies on the Psalms*, Forschungen zur Kirchen- und Dogmengeschichte 47 (Göttingen, Germany: Vandenhoeck & Ruprecht, 1990), 17–19.

71. Louis Ellies du Pin, *Nouvelle Bibliothèque des Auteurs Ecclésiastiques*, vol. 2 (Paris, 1687–1689); Marcel Richard, "Les Homélies d'Astérius sur les Psaumes IV–VII," *Revue Biblique* 44 (1935), 548–558; Richard, ed., *Asterii Sophistae Commentariorum In Psalmos Quae Supersunt Accedunt Aliquot Homiliae Anonymae* (Oslo: A.W. Brøgger, 1962). For a full discussion of the scholarly debate over the authenticity of these homilies, see Kinzig, 22–37.

72. Kinzig presents a convincing argument that these Homilies on the Psalms were *not* the work of Asterius Sophistes and were probably written by a pro-Nicene author in western Syria or Palestine between 385 and 410 (Kinzig, 227). Others, including Richard, Auf der Maur (Hansjörg auf der Maur, *Die Osterhomilien des Asterios Sophistes als Quelle für die Geschichte der Osterfeier* [Trier: Paulinus-Verlag, 1967], 8) and Talley, accept their Asterian authenticity; for this reason, the evidence they contain is included.

73. Auf der Maur maintains that it was likely either Cappadocia or Syria, probably Cappadocia (Auf der Maur, 9).

74. Rousseau, 100.

75. Basil of Caesarea, *Ep.* 51.2.

76. Philostorgius, *The Ecclesiastical History of Philostorgius Compiled by Photius, Patriarch of Constantinople*, 2.15; 4.4 .

77. Kinzig, 12.

78. Cantalamessa, 167.

79. Asterius Sophistes, *In Psalmum V Homilia VI seu in feriam II infra Octauam Paschae*, 4.

80. Ibid., 10.

81. Asterius Sophistes, *Homilia in feriam V infra Octauam Paschae* 5.

82. Talley, *Origins*, 56–57.

83. Basil of Caesarea, *On the Spirit* 27.66, *NPNF*, Series 2, vol. 8, 42–43.

84. Gregory of Nazianzus, *Oration 41 On Pentecost* 10, *NPNF*, Series 2, vol. 7, 382. According to Bernardi, Gregory preached this sermon to a congregation of monks in Constantinople on the Day of Pentecost, June 9, 379 (Bernardi, 157).

85. Ibid. 5, *NPNF*, 380–381.

86. Ibid. 6, *NPNF*, 381.

87. Ibid. 10, *NPNF*, 383.

88. Ibid.11, *NPNF*, 383; emphasis added.

89. Gregory of Nyssa, *In Sanctam Pentecosten*, *GNO* 10.2.3, 288.27–28.

90. According to Daniélou, Gregory preached this sermon on May 28, 388 (Daniélou, "Chronologie," 372).

91. Gregory of Nyssa, *In Sanctam Pentecosten*, *GNO* 10.2.3, 287.5–10.

92. Bernardi, 289.

93. Moutsoulas, 343: *Il rappelle l'état de l'homme après la chute, son éloignement de Dieu et l'amour de Dieu qui, progressivement, a ramené la vie humaine à la connaissance de la Verité. D'abord nous avons la révélation par les prophètes et la Loi, qu'il n'y a qu'un Dieu. Ensuite par l'Évangile il nous est révélé la Personne du Fils unique. Enfin a eu lieu dans l'Église la révélation de l'Esprit Saint «dans lequel se trouve la vie» (cf. P.G. 46, 697AB). Par le souffle puissant de l'Esprit «les forces spirituelles du mal se sont dispersées et les disciples qui se trouvaient dans la*

chambre haute ont été remplis de force divine» (697c).

94.   Gregory of Nyssa, *In Sanctam Pentecosten, GNO* 10.2.3, 290.3–4.

95.   Ibid., *GNO* 10.2.3, 288.25–26.

96.   Therefore, as the Holy Spirit says, "Today, if you hear his voice, do not harden your hearts as in the rebellion, as on the day of testing in the wilderness, where your ancestors put me to the test, though they had seen my works for forty years. Therefore I was angry with that generation, and I said, 'They always go astray in their hearts, and they have not known my ways.' As in my anger I swore, 'They will not enter my rest.'" (NRSV).

97.   Gregory of Nyssa, *In Sanctam Pentecosten, GNO* 10.2.3, 290.5–291.4.

98.   Ibid., *GNO* 10.2.3, 291.12–13.

99.   Ibid., *GNO* 10.2.3, 291.4–5.

100.   Ibid., *GNO* 10.2.3, 291.19–27.

101.   Ibid., *GNO* 10.2.3, 292.8–11.

102.   Daniélou, "Grégoire," 663–664.

103.   The Greek title is translated "For the day called ἐπισῳζομένη according to the local custom of Cappadocia, which is the Ascension of Our Lord Jesus Christ."

104.   Eusebius, *De solemnitate paschali* 5. Eusebius's *Vita Constantini* 4.64 also mentions this observance.

105.   *Itinerarium Egeriae* 43.1.

106.   Daniélou, "Grégoire," 663: *Mais le contexte paraît bien marquer qu'il fait allusion à la célébration du mystère de l'Ascension le cinquantième jour, puisqu'il souligne que la* μεσηπεντεκόστη *se trouve au milieu des deux grandes fêtes de Pâques et de l'Ascension.*

107.   *In Mesopentecosten* 3.4. Emphasis added.

108.   Cabié, 100.

109.   Datema, *Amphilochius,* xx–xxi.

110.   Cabié, 158–159.

111.   Daniélou, "Grégoire," 664.

112.   Chromatius of Aquileia, *De ascensione domini* 8.1 states explicitly that the feast is happening on the fortieth day after Easter.

113.   Filastrius of Brescia, *Diversarum haereseon liber* 140.2; 149.3. For a discussion of this early evidence from Northern Italy, see Martin Connell, "The Liturgical Year in Northern Italy (365–450)" (Ph.D. diss., University of Notre Dame, 1994), 135–136.

114.   Talley, *Origins,* 68.

115.   John Chrysostom, Homily 19; *Apostolic Constitutions* 5.20.2.

116.   Daniélou, "Gregoire," 663.

117.   Talley, *Origins,* 168.

118.   Ibid., 169.

119.   Athanasius of Alexandria, Letter 12, *NPNF* Series 2, vol. 4, 538.

120.   Talley, *Origins,* 170. That Rome observed a forty-day Lent is directly attested by later in the fourth century in Jerome's Epistle 24.4 to Marcella (384 C.E.) and Pope Siricius's letter to Himerius of Tarragona in 385 (Maxwell E. Johnson, "Preparation for Pascha? Lent in Christian Antiquity," in *Between Memory and Hope: Readings on the Liturgical Year,* ed. Maxwell E. Johnson [Collegeville, MN: The Liturgical Press, 2000], 210).

121. Talley, *Origins*, 171.
122. *Apostolic Constitutions*, 5.13.
123. Talley, *Origins*, 171.
124. Egeria, *Itinerarium Egeriae* 27.1.
125. Sozomon, *The Ecclesiastical History* 7.19, *NPNF*, Series 2, vol. 2, 390.
126. Ruether, 179; Bernardi, 204.
127. Gregory of Nazianzus, *Oration 40 On Holy Baptism* 30, *NPNF*, Series 2, vol. 7, 371.
128. Gregory of Nyssa, *In XL Martyres Ib*, *GNO* 10.1.2, 152.11–13.
129. Asterius of Amaseia, *Oratio in principium jejuniorum* 2.1.
130. Bernardi, 74–76; Paul Fedwick agrees that it was an Easter homily but sees no evidence to date it to 372 (Paul J. Fedwick, "A Chronology of the Life and Works of Basil of Caesarea," in *Basil of Caesarea: Christian, Humanist, Ascetic: A Sixteen-Hundredth Anniversary Symposium*, Part One, ed. Paul Jonathan Fedwick [Toronto: Pontifical Institute of Mediaeval Studies, 1981], 9, n. 37).
131. Basil, *In ebriosos* 1.
132. Bernardi, 70–72.
133. Basil of Caesarea, *De jejunio* I.7. Emphasis added.
134. Ibid. 10.
135. Ibid., *De jejunio* II.4.
136. Ibid. 7.
137. Bernardi, 45–46.
138. Basil of Caesarea, *De jejunio* II.8.
139. Bernardi, 46.
140. Asterius of Amaseia, *Oratio in principium jejuniorum* 8.4.
141. Ibid. 8.2–3.
142. Ibid. 9.4.
143. Ibid. 10.1.
144. Ibid. 11.1.
145. Ibid.12.2.
146. Bernardi, 46.
147. Basil of Caesarea, *De jejunio* I.1.
148. Ibid. 3.
149. Ibid. 4–5.
150. Ibid., 4.
151. Ibid. 6.
152. Ibid. 10.
153. Basil of Caesarea, *De jejunio* II.1.
154. Ibid. 3.
155. Ibid. 4.
156. Ibid. 5.
157. Ibid. 7.
158. Ibid. 8.
159. See above, p. 37.
160. Gregory of Nazianzus, *Oration 1 On Easter and His Reluctance* 7, *NPNF*, Series 2, vol. 7, 204.

161.   Gregory of Nazianzus, *Oration 45 Second Paschal Oration* 4; Amphilochius of
        Iconium, *De recens baptizatis* 4; *In diem Sabbati Sancti* 1.

162.   Ibid. 26–27. See p. 88 for the quotation from the Christmas sermon.

163.   Talley, *Origins*, 68.

164.   See pp. 39ff.

Chapter 3

The Nativity/Incarnation Cycle

The evidence from around the Mediterranean indicates that, generally speaking, by the middle of the fourth century, the churches of the East feasted Christ's birth and baptism on the same day, January 6,[1] while the churches of the West observed December 25 as their Nativity feast.[2] By the last quarter of the century, the calendars of most churches in both East and West included both feasts. Scholars have explained the adoption of Christmas in the East and Epiphany in the West by suggesting that during the latter half of the fourth century, after the Peace of Constantine had made the commerce of Christian ideas legal and, consequently, safer, the churches of the two halves of the Roman Empire exchanged nativity feasts. The Eastern churches divided their unitive feast celebrating the birth and baptism of Jesus and transferred the nativity commemoration to the feast on December 25. Epiphany then became the feast celebrating the baptism of Jesus, as it is today. The Western churches added January 6 as a second nativity observance, eventually distinguishing between the two feasts by celebrating the visit of the magi, which had once been part of a unitive feast celebrating all facets of the nativity story, on the feast of the Epiphany on January 6. As far as it goes, this is a useful and accurate summary, although it obscures somewhat the complexity of these developments. In this chapter we will examine the Cappadocian sources in order to ascertain as clearly as possible if and when this "feast exchange" took place there, under what circumstances and with what consequences for the fourth-century Cappadocian liturgical calendar.

Two Incarnation Feasts

The earliest evidence of a Christian feast observed on January 6 comes from Clement of Alexandria, who says that some Basilidians, an early second-century Gnostic Christian group in Alexandria, celebrated the baptism of Christ on January 6.[3] There is no further mention of a feast on this day until the middle of the fourth century. Curiously, it comes from the West; Ammianus Marcellinus reports that Emperor Julian attended church in Gaul on Epiphany, "in the month of January" of 361.[4] Cappadocian sources are among the earliest fourth-century Eastern documents to contain evidence of the January 6 feast, and while scholars believe that Epiphany pre-dated Christmas in this region, the two feasts appear in these sources at roughly the same time.

John Chrysostom, preaching in Antioch on December 25, c. 386, gives us fairly precise information about the institution of the feast there—or at least about how long *he* had known about the feast. He says, "It is scarcely ten years, in fact, since this day has been made manifest and known to us. At present the feast is not everywhere kept, for I know that even now many are still discussing it among themselves."[5] Our Cappadocian and Pontic friends were not among those who were still debating the feast's merits; it is clear that by the mid-380s, Constantinople, Nyssa and Amaseia celebrated both Christmas and Epiphany, although, unfortunately, they have not left us such precise information about when this happened. Citing Gregory of Nazianzus' self-designation as the ἔξαρχος of the Theophany feast,[6] many scholars credit him with instituting Christmas in Constantinople during his brief tenure as bishop there. Botte, for example, writes:

> We possess two homilies of Gregory of Nazianzus, one on Christmas, the other on Epiphany, preached at Constantinople. At the time of his short stay in this Church, therefore, he celebrated the two feasts there. But that of Christmas is of recent institution, and Gregory calls himself the ἔξαρχος of this feast. It is he who instituted it, and it is interesting to note that this innovation is not without relation to the anti-Arian reaction, just as at Alexandria it will coincide with the anti-Nestorian movement.[7]

We will return to the question of the relationship of the adoption of Christmas to the doctrinal controversies in which Cappadocian church leaders were involved. First, however, it is necessary to address the question of the precise meaning of ἔξαρχος for Gregory. The term has several meanings. Botte and the other scholars listed above interpret it as "founder." However, as Susan Roll points out, other scholars, such as McArthur, Theodorou and Talley,[8] maintain that it could also mean merely "leader" and that "Gregory was presiding at the liturgy of an already established feast."[9] Roll herself does not offer an opinion, but she does cite Talley's convincing assessment of this matter. Talley writes:

What can be said with reasonable assurance is that it seems highly unlikely that the festival would have been adopted from Rome under an Arian emperor. Therefore, if not adopted since the death of Valens, it would have had to be a very early feature of the Byzantine liturgy, given the brevity of the episodes of orthodoxy in the imperial city between Constantine and Theodosius. If the institution of Christmas at Rome had as much to do with Constantine's solar piety as has been urged by some, one would expect him to have pressed for the festival in his new capital, but of that we have no evidence whatsoever. If, on the contrary, we are to look for the introduction of the festival of December 25 after the fall of Valens, then the interpretation of *exarchos* becomes somewhat academic. If Gregory Nazianzen did not preside at the first celebration of Christmas in Constantinople in 380, that occasion was no more than the second such celebration of the feast.[10]

However, was Gregory of Nazianzus really the trendsetter in this instance? Talley implies that this was the case when he writes, "From the time of the restoration of orthodoxy with the accession of Theodosius, then, the observance of the nativity festival on December 25 extended smoothly and swiftly from Constantinople across Cappadocia to Antioch."[11] Is it possible, however, that Basil had already introduced it at Caesarea and that, therefore, the extension of the December 25 feast was from *Cappadocia* northwest to Constantinople and southeast to Antioch? His homily *In sanctam Christi generationem*[12] had to have been preached at least one year earlier than Gregory's sermon, since Basil died on January 1, 379. But was this sermon preached on December 25 or January 6? Fedwick dates it to January 6, sometime during Basil's ordained ministry—between the years 363 and 378. The sermon itself does not say; Fedwick's determination seems to be based only on what happened in "the East" generally, that is, events surrounding the incarnation that we now associate with *two* feasts were celebrated on the same day—January 6—until the end of the fourth century.[13] Botte and Talley disagree, maintaining that this sermon was preached on December 25.[14] Let us examine the text in search of clues.

Basil begins his remarks with an exhortation, "Let the birth of Christ, the fitting and first and peculiar [birth] of his deity, be honored in silence; rather let us also order our thoughts not to seek nor be curious about these things."[15] In this case, Basil is not out to spoil everyone's fun; he is beginning this sermon with anti-Arian sentiment. Basil warns his congregation to avoid trying to understand the mystery of the incarnation in terms of human reason. He says:

But the Father existed, and the Son was begotten. Do not say "when?" but pass over the question; do not inquire "how?" for the answer is impossible. For the "when," on the one hand, [is] temporal; the "how," on the other hand, produces a snare with regard to the bodily means of the birth. I am able to say from the scripture "as a reflection from the glory and as an image from the prototype" (Heb. 1.3). Nevertheless, since such a word of answer does not stay the inquisitiveness of your reasonings, I appeal to the inexpressibility of the glory, and I confess that the manner of the divine birth is inconceivable by reasonings and unutterable in human words. Do not say "if he was begotten, he did not exist," and do not maliciously grasp vulgar understandings of words, falsifying the truth from the examples here and defiling the theology. He was begotten, I have said, in order that I might proclaim his origin and source, not in order that I might later refute the Only-begotten.[16]

The silence Basil seeks is more an attitude of heart than adherence to a "gag order." After a long meditation on the incomprehensibility of the incarnation, during which he cites Isaiah 7 and 9, Matthew 1.18–2.9 and portions of Luke 1 and 2 to muse on the virginity of Mary, Jesus' various appellations, the Magi, the star, the shepherds and the angels, he encourages joyful, *unquestioning* noise:

Who is so sluggish in soul, who is so ungrateful, as not to rejoice and exult and brighten up at the present circumstances? A communal feast of all creation; it presents the supramundane things to the world; it sends the archangels to Zachariah and to Mary and establishes the choruses of angels who say: "Glory to God in the highest and on earth peace, good will among humans" (Lk. 2.14). Stars run about from heaven; Magi are moved from the Gentiles; earth receives in a cave; no one is uncontributing, no one is ungrateful. Let *us* also utter some sound of exultation; let us give a name to our feast, Theophany; let us feast the salvation of the world, the birthday (τὴν γενέθλιον ἡμέραν) of the humanity. Today the condemnation of Adam has been abolished.[17]

The phrase "let us appoint a name to our feast, Theophany; let us feast the salvation of the world, the birthday of the humanity" raises two questions pertinent to our discussion. First, to which feast does Theophany (Θεοφάνια) refer? Second, does "let us give a name to our feast" (ὄνομα θώμεθα τῇ ἑορτῇ ἡμῶν) indicate that this feast was an innovation in need of an appellation?

With regard to the question of festal names, Mossay points out that in the fourth-century Cappadocian sources there are four terms—ἡ Ἐπιφάνια, τὰ Φῶτα, τὰ Θεοφάνια, and τὰ Γενέθλια—used to refer to the two feasts of December 25 and January 6. He also suggests that there was an evolution of terminology. He writes, "At a time when Christmas takes the names of Theophany or Nativity, that is to say around 380, the term Epiphany designating the feast of January 6 is supplanted by the expression feast of the Lights."[18] So if the December 25 feast did not take the name Theophany until around 380, Basil's earlier use of the term must have referred to the January 6 feast. Talley does not read the data this way. As mentioned above, he believes Basil's sermon was for the December 25 feast, and he writes:

> In Cappadocia the situation is similar to that in Constantinople, the nativity festival on December 25 is called 'Theophany' (but sometimes *Genethlia*) and the festival of January 6 celebrates Christ's baptism and is called 'The Feast of Lights.' This was the case with Gregory of Nyssa and Basil, as well as others in Cappadocia. Amphilochius of Iconium, in a Christmas sermon (PG 39.3644), uses only *ta genethlia* to designate the festival. The Byzantine tradition finally settled on that title for the December feast, using both *Theophania* and *ta phôta* of that in January in the typika of Hagia Sophia in the ninth and tenth centuries.[19]

So for Talley, the evolution of the term Theophany moves in the opposite direction than that suggested by Mossay. The second question raised above—that of Basil's suggestion "let us give a name to our feast"—supports Talley's reading. This phrase makes much more sense in reference to a new feast than to the renaming of an already-established festival. In addition, the sermon is entirely about events surrounding Christ's birth; his baptism is not mentioned.

However, it seems that the only thing we can say for sure from the text is that this sermon was for the day on which Basil's community celebrated Christ's birth. Are there other sources that might help answer the question of on which day that celebration was held? In late 375 or early 376, Basil wrote to his friend Amphilochius of Iconium to thank him for some gifts. He writes:

> Every day that brings me a letter from you is a feast day, the very greatest of feast days. And when symbols of the feast are brought, what can I call it but a feast of feasts, as the old law used to speak of Sabbath of Sabbaths? I thank the Lord that you are quite well, and that you have celebrated the commemoration of the œconomy of salvation in a Church at peace.[20]

What was this "commemoration of the œconomy of salvation" (τῆς σωτηρίου οἰκονομίας τὴν ἀνάμνησιν)? F. Loofs leans toward January 6, because he assumes that the December 25 feast had not yet been adopted in "the East" at this point.[21] At some point during his episcopate, Amphilochius preached a homily on the birthday feast (τὰ Γενέθλια) of Christ; the use of the term γενέθλια and the fact that the sermon is entirely about the events surrounding Christ's birth and not at all about Christ's baptism indicate that this sermon was intended for the December 25 feast. Would he have already known this feast in 375/376? Datema thinks not; he dates the homily to later in Amphilochius's ministry because Amphilochius describes this feast as "all-venerable" and "all-praised," a status that a feast would not enjoy until it had been around awhile. Citing the "fact" that "it is only toward the year 380 that the feast of Christmas is instituted in Cappadocia and in neighboring regions,"[22] Datema concludes that this homily must be from the 380s or 390s. A bit further on in Basil's letter to Amphilochius, he writes:

> Do come to see me while I am yet upon this earth. Act in accordance with your own wishes and with my most earnest prayers. I may be allowed to be astonished at the meaning of your blessings, inasmuch as you have mysteriously wished me a vigorous old age. By your lamps you rouse me to nightly toil; and by your sweet meats you seem to pledge yourself securely that all my body is in good case. But there is no munching for me at my time of life, for my teeth have long ago been worn away by time and bad health.[23]

Does the fact that Amphilochius sent Basil lamps (λαμπῆναι)[24] and sweet meats (τραγήματα) as "symbols of the feast" (σύμβολα ἑορτῆς) help us to identify the feast in question? Unfortunately, it does not, because gift-giving was also practiced at other festivals. For example, Gregory of Nyssa wrote a short meditation on the relationship between the seasons and two Christian feasts as an Easter gift to Eusebius, Bishop of Chalcis in Coele-Syria, writing, "Why, since it is the custom in these general holidays (ἐν ταῖς πανδήμοις ταύταις ἱερομηνίαις) for us to take every way to show the affection harbored in our hearts, and we thought it only right not to leave you without the homage of our gifts, but to lay before your lofty and high-minded soul the scanty offerings of our poverty."[25] Gregory also wrote *On the Making of Man*, intended as a supplement to Basil's *Haexameron*, as an Easter gift to his brother Peter, since "the holy Eastertide demands the accustomed gift of love...."[26] Gregory of Nazianzus also participated in this custom of giving gifts at Easter. Two of his letters to Theodore of Tyana in Cappadocia Secunda, are thank-you notes for Theodore's gifts.[27] Gregory reciprocated by sending his prayers and a copy of the *Philocalia of Origen*, which he and Basil had compiled together in 358–359.

Unfortunately, Basil's *Exhortatoria ad sanctum baptisma*, which Bernardi dates to January 6, 371 and Fedwick assigns to January 5 or 6 sometime during the period of 363 to 378,[28] does not help to answer the question either. It gives much information about baptism but mentions neither a December 25 nor a January 6 feast. In fact, the only feast it *does* mention is the Pascha, as discussed in Chapter Two. In his eulogy on Basil, Gregory of Nazianzus mentions a confrontation between Basil and Valens when Valens attended church on the feast of the Epiphany in 372, but he does not give us any information about the celebration, other than that the church was very crowded and the psalmody was chanted very loudly.[29]

It is not until the sermons of the two Gregorys that we find enough evidence to prove for sure that the churches in this area were now observing feasts on both December 25 and January 6. Both Gregorys distinguish between the two feasts. In his *Oration 38 On the Theophany, or Birthday of Christ*, which Ruether dates to December 25, 379,[30] Gregory of Nazianzus says "Christ is Born, glorify ye Him"[31] and after briefly mentioning Christ's ascension and second coming, he calls himself back to the topic at hand:

> Of these on a future occasion; for the present the Festival is the Theophany or Birthday, for it is called both, two titles being given to the one thing. For God was manifested to man by birth. On the one hand Being, and eternally Being, of the Eternal Being, above cause and word, for there was no word before The Word; and on the other hand for our sakes also Becoming, that He Who gives us our being might restore us by His Incarnation, when we had by wickedness fallen from wellbeing. The name Theophany is given to it in reference to the Manifestation, and that of Birthday in respect of His Birth. This is our present Festival; it is this which we are celebrating to-day, the Coming of God to Man....[32]

The fact that Gregory refers to both the manifestation and the birthday might lead us to believe that the community at Constantinople still celebrated both the birth and the baptism on the same day; however, later in the sermon, Gregory indicates that this is not the case. He says:

> A little later on you will see Jesus submitting to be purified in the River Jordan for my Purification, or rather, sanctifying the waters by His Purification (for indeed He had no need of purification Who taketh away the sin of the world) and the heavens cleft asunder, and witness borne to him by the Spirit That is of one nature with Him; you shall see Him tempted and conquering and served by Angels, and healing every sickness and every disease, and giving life to the dead (O that He would give life to you who are dead because of your heresy), and driving out demons, sometimes Himself, sometimes by his disciples; and feeding vast multitudes with a few loaves;

and walking dryshod upon the seas; and being betrayed and crucified, and crucify-
ing with Himself my sin; offered as a Lamb, and offering as a Priest; as a Man buried in the grave, and as God rising again; and then ascending, and to come again in
His own glory. Why what a multitude of high festivals there are in each of the mysteries of the Christ; all of which have one completion, namely, my perfection and
return to the first condition of Adam.[33]

This is not a catalogue of the "high festivals" observed in Constantinople; it seems to be a list—more or less chronological—of events from Matthew's account of Christ's life and ministry. However, the phrase "a little
later on" does suggest that the first event listed—that of Jesus' baptism by
John—will be observed at a later date. Gregory's next paragraph confirms
this, because it tells us what the *present* festival is about:

Now then I pray you accept His Conception, and leap before Him; if not like John
from the womb, yet like David, because of the resting of the Ark. Revere the enrollment on account of which thou wast written in heaven, and adore the Birth by
which thou wast written in heaven, and adore the Birth by which thou wast loosed
from the chains of thy birth, and honour little Bethlehem, which hath led thee back
to Paradise; and worship the manger through which thou, being without sense, wast
fed by the Word.[34]

In addition, Gregory provides us with another sermon, which most
scholars date to the following January 6,[35] that addresses Christ's baptism
specifically and differentiates that feast from the one celebrating Christ's
birth. In his *Oration 39 On the Holy Lights*, Gregory says:

At His birth we duly kept Festival, both I, the leader of the Feast, and you, and all
that is in the world and above the world. With the Star we ran, and with the Magi we
worshipped, and with the Shepherds we were illuminated, and with the Angels we
glorified Him, and with Simeon we took Him up in our arms, and with Anna the
aged and chaste we made our responsive confession. And thanks be to Him who
came to His own in the guise of a stranger, because He glorified the stranger. Now,
we come to another action of Christ, and another mystery. I cannot restrain my
pleasure; I am rapt into God. Almost like John I proclaim good tidings; for though I
be not a Forerunner, yet am I from the desert. Christ is illumined, let us shine forth
with Him. Christ is baptized, let us descend with Him that we may also ascend with
Him.[36]

A couple of years later, Gregory of Nyssa, in his January 6, 383[37] homily
In diem luminum, also distinguishes between the feasts and their themes. He
says, "Christ, then, was born as it were a few days ago—He Whose generation was before all things, sensible and intellectual. To-day He is baptized by

John that He might cleanse him who was defiled, that He might bring the Spirit from above and exalt man to heaven, that he who had fallen might be raised up and he who had cast him down might be put to shame."[38] On the feast of St. Stephen, in a homily that Daniélou dates to 386,[39] Gregory puts the Nativity celebration in relation to the day honoring the first martyr:

> How lovely is the inspiration exhibited by those who are good, and how sweet is the joy which they disclose! See, we acquire a feast from a feast and grace from grace. Yesterday the Lord of the universe welcomed us whereas today it is the imitator of the Lord. How are they related to each other? One assumed human nature on our behalf while the other shed it for his Lord. One accepted the cave of this life for us, and the other left it for him. One was wrapped in swaddling clothes for us, and the other was stoned for him. One destroyed death, and the other scorned it.[40]

In another sermon preached on the feast of St. Stephen in 386,[41] Asterius of Amaseia also places the Nativity feast and the saint's day in relation to one another:

> How truly holy and good [is] the cycle of events that gladden us! For feast succeeds to feast, and festal gathering overtakes festal gathering; and we are called from prayer into prayer, and the honoring of the servant overtakes the Theophany of the Lord. But whether someone looks to the birth yesterday of the one who was brought into the world through flesh and is forever in accordance with divinity, or to the martyrdom of that one, which indeed the noble servant today has undertaken, he will find many and various events, but one goal, that *we* might be taught godliness. So then yesterday we learned through the cyclical [ἐγκυκλίου] and customary [συν-ήθους] feast that the Savior of the world was born, and the fleshless one clothed himself in flesh, and the bodiless one put on a body, then that he also accepted sufferings for our sake and was lifted up on the tree not for the sake of some other or for our provision. But today we see the noble combatant being stoned to death for his sake, in order that he might repay the grace with blood for the sake of blood.[42]

So, by the mid-380s, the celebration of Christ's birth was a separate feast, held on December 25, in Constantinople, Nyssa and Amaseia, as well as in Iconium by the 390s. Of Caesarea we cannot be as certain. If Basil's letter to Amphilochius is referring to the December 25 feast and if Basil's sermon on the birthday of Christ was for that feast, this would mean that *Basil*, not Gregory of Nazianzus, was the first to institute it in this region, even if, as seems likely, Gregory was the one who initially brought it to Constantinople.

Shifting Festal Themes

Because we do not know for sure for which feast Basil intended *In sanctam Christi generationem,* and we have little other information about the celebration of Epiphany in Cappadocia before Christmas arrived,[43] it is difficult to determine if and how the content of the January 6 feast shifted when the December 25 feast was adopted. As mentioned above, Basil's *Exhortatoria ad sanctum baptisma* does not situate itself on any particular feast. However, if Bernardi and Fedwick are correct in assigning it to Epiphany, and if Bernardi is correct in dating it to 371, we may be able to gather a few clues about what happened on January 6 in Caesarea in the years before the adoption of the December 25 feast.

First, it is essential to note that this sermon contains nothing at all about the birth of Christ. Neither is the baptism of Christ its theme. Basil does speak generally about the baptism administered by John, but only in order to contrast it with the baptism administered by the church. In so doing, he tells us what scripture readings were appointed for the day. He says:

> John proclaimed a baptism of repentance, and all Judea went out to him; the Lord proclaims a baptism of adoption, and who of the ones who have hoped in him will not listen? That was the elementary baptism; this is perfective. That was a retreat of sin; this is appropriation by God. The proclamation of John was of one man, and he drew everyone to repentance; but do you, being taught through prophets—"Wash yourself, become clean" (Is. 1.16)—, being admonished through psalms—"Draw near to him and be enlightened" (Ps. 33.6)—, being evangelized through apostles— "Repent and be baptized, each of you, in the name of the Lord Jesus Christ for forgiveness of sins, and you will gain the promise of the Holy Spirit" (Acts 2.38)—, being received by the Lord himself, who says: "Come to me, all who are weary and heavy laden, and I will give you rest" (Mt. 11.28) (for all these things have come together today for the public reading)—do you hesitate and deliberate and continually delay?[44]

The sermon is entirely about the dangers and folly of hesitating about, deliberating over and continually delaying baptism. In the passage quoted in Chapter 2,[45] Basil says that baptism may be received at any time, although the Pascha is the most suitable occasion. On the other hand, the sermon is full of warnings not to wait much beyond the next Easter. Basil asks:

> A tempter through life, a spy until old age, when will you become a Christian? When will we point you out as ours? Last year you waited for the present time, now again you await the following [year]. Be on guard lest you be found making prom-

ises longer than [your] life. You do not know what the following [year] will bring
forth; do not promise things [that are] not yours.[46]

We also know that this sermon was preached on the day on which candi-
dates for baptism were enrolled. Basil issues the following invitation:

> Therefore, come now to me, transfer yourself wholly to the Lord; freely give your
> name; be registered with the Church. The soldier is reckoned by the registers; the
> athlete contends having registered himself; the citizen is reckoned having been en-
> rolled as a citizen by fellow tribesmen. You are responsible to all these things, as a
> soldier of Christ, as an athlete of piety, as having citizenship in heaven. Be regis-
> tered in this book, in order that you might be translated into the one above.[47]

By the time both feasts were unquestionably included in the calendars in
question, the Feast of Lights on January 6 focused on Christ's baptism. We
have already noted the differentiation Gregory of Nazianzus made between
the content of the two feasts. *Oration 39 On the Holy Lights* begins:

> Again My Jesus, and again a mystery, not deceitful nor disorderly, nor belonging to
> Greek error or drunkenness (for so I call their solemnities, and so I think will every
> man of sound sense); but a mystery lofty and divine, and allied to the Glory above.
> For the Holy Day of the Lights, to which we have come, and which we are cele-
> brating to-day, has for its origin the Baptism of my Christ, the True Light That
> lighteneth every man that cometh into the world, and effecteth my purification, and
> assists that light which we received from the beginning from Him from above, but
> which we darkened and confused by sin.[48]

The rest of the sermon contrasts this feast with those of the Greeks, contrasts it with the Christian feast celebrating Christ's birth, discusses Christ's
baptism, as well as the different prefigurations of baptism found in the Hebrew scriptures and the different kinds of New Testament and present-day
baptisms known by Christians. Gregory concludes his remarks with a reit-
eration of the day's main theme:

> But let us venerate to-day the Baptism of Christ; and let us keep the feast well, not
> in pampering the belly, but rejoicing the spirit. And how shall we luxuriate? "Wash
> you, make you clean." ...Anyhow be purified, and you shall be clean (for God re-
> joices in nothing so much as in the amendment and salvation of man, on whose be-
> half is every discourse and every Sacrament), that you may be like lights in the
> world, a quickening force to all other men; that you may stand as perfect lights be-
> side That great Light, and may learn the mystery of the illumination of Heaven, en-
> lightened by the Trinity more purely and clearly, of Which even now you are

receiving in a measure the One Ray from the One Godhead in Christ Jesus our Lord....[49]

Gregory's *Oration* 40 *On Holy Baptism*, preached the following day, provides more glimpses into his interpretation of the feast of the Holy Lights but focuses more on the baptism of Christians than on that of Christ. He begins:

> Yesterday we kept high Festival on the illustrious Day of the Holy Lights; for it was fitting that rejoicings should be kept for our Salvation, and that far more than for weddings and birthdays, and namedays, and house-warmings, and registrations of children, and anniversaries, and all the other festivities that men observe for their earthly friends. And now to-day let us discourse briefly concerning Baptism, and the benefits which accrue to us therefrom, even though our discourse yesterday spoke of it cursorily; partly because the time pressed us hard, and partly because the sermon had to avoid tediousness.[50]

Gregory of Nyssa also differentiated between the content of the two feasts, as mentioned above. He says:

> Therefore let us leave the other matters of the Scriptures for other occasions, and abide by the topic set before us, offering, as far as we may, the gifts that are proper and fitting for the feast: for each festival demands its own treatment. So we welcome a marriage with wedding songs; for mourning we bring the due offering with funeral strains; in times of business we speak seriously, at times of festivity we relax the concentration and strain of our minds; but each time we keep free from disturbance by things that are alien to its character.[51]

He concludes this sermon, "And now we have spoken sufficiently for the holy subject of the day, which the circling year brings to us at appointed periods." From the passage cited above, we know that Gregory held the baptism of Christ to be "holy subject" of this particular day, whereas Christ's birth was the suitable topic "a few days ago."[52]

In addition to serving as a commemoration of Christ's baptism at the hands of John, the Feast of Lights was a major baptismal occasion for the Christians of this area. Although Basil claims that Pascha is the best time for baptism, the Feast of Lights is the occasion for which baptismal homilies survive from Basil and both Gregorys. Gregory of Nazianzus urges the unbaptized members of his congregation not to delay baptism. He says:

> Let us then be baptized that we may win the victory.... Let us be baptized today, that we suffer not violence to-morrow; and let us not put off the blessing as if it

were an injury, nor wait till we get more wicked that more may be forgiven us; and let us not become sellers and traffickers of Christ, lest we become more heavily burdened than we are able to bear.... While thou art still master of thy thoughts run to the Gift.[53]

Gregory of Nyssa's January 6 homily urges the *faithful* to bring the uninitiated to the font:

The time, then, has come, and bears in its course the remembrance of holy mysteries, purifying man, – mysteries which purge out from soul and body even that sin which is hard to cleanse away, and which bring us back to that fairness of our first estate which God, the best of artificers, impressed upon us. There it is that you, the initiated people, are gathered together; and you bring also that people who have not made trial of them, leading, like good father, by careful guidance, the uninitiated to the perfect reception of faith.[54]

Gregory of Nyssa's homily also gives us some glimpses of baptismal meanings and practices, as well as some information of Gregory's sacramental theology in general. He explains:

Baptism, then, is a purification from sins, a remission of trespasses, a cause of renovation and regeneration. By regeneration, understand regeneration conceived in thought, not discerned by bodily sight.... And this gift it is not the water that bestows (for in that case it were a thing more exalted than all creation), but the command of God, and the visitation of the Spirit that comes sacramentally to set us free. But water serves to express the cleansing.... Despise not, therefore, the Divine laver, nor think lightly of it, as a common thing, on account of the use of water. For the power that operates is mighty, and wonderful are the things that are wrought thereby. For this holy altar, too, by which I stand, is stone, ordinary in its nature, nowise different from the other slabs of stone that build our houses and adorn our pavements; but seeing that it was consecrated to the service of God, and received the benediction, it is a holy table, an altar undefiled, no longer touched by the hands of all, but of the priests alone, and that with reverence. The bread again is at first common bread, but when the sacramental action consecrates it, it is called and becomes the Body of Christ. So with the sacramental oil; so with the wine: though before the benediction they are of little value, each of them, after the sanctification bestowed by the Spirit, has its several operations. The same power of the word, again, also makes the priest venerable and honourable, separated, by the new blessing bestowed upon him, from his community with the mass of men.[55]

Gregory then responds to a question about the fact that in baptism one is immersed three times. His answer gives us a picture of how baptism was administered. He says:

> We recognize four elements, of which the world is composed, which every one knows even if their names are not spoken; but if it is well, for the sake of the more simple, to tell you their names, they are fire and air, earth and water. Now our God and Saviour, in fulfilling the Dispensation for our sakes, went beneath the fourth of these, the earth, that He might raise up life from thence. And we in receiving Baptism, in imitation of our Lord and teacher and Guide, are not indeed buried in the earth (for this is the shelter of the body that is entirely dead, covering the infirmity and decay of our nature), but coming to the element akin to earth, to water, we conceal ourselves in that as the Saviour did in the earth: and by doing this thrice we represent for ourselves that grace of the Resurrection which was wrought in three days: and this we do, not receiving the sacrament in silence, but while there are spoken over us the Names of the Three Sacred Persons on Whom we believed, in Whom we also hope, from Whom comes to us both the fact of our present and the fact of our future existence. [56]

But this was not the *only* suitable day for baptism. In trying to persuade the uninitiated among his listeners to take the plunge, Gregory of Nazianzus writes: "Every time is suitable for your ablution, since any time may be your death. With Paul I shout to you with that loud voice, 'Behold now is the accepted time; behold Now is the day of salvation;' and that Now does not point to any one time, but is every present moment."[57] Later in this homily Gregory continues to encourage immediate response to the call to baptism, but in exposing the folly of excuses given, he also informs us that Easter and Pentecost were other baptismal occasions. He says:

> Therefore since you have heard these words, come forward to it, and be enlightened, and your faces shall not be ashamed through missing the Grace. Receive then the Enlightenment in due season, that darkness pursue you not, and catch you, and sever you from the Illumining.... And consider how Solomon reproves you who are too idle or lethargic, saying, How long wilt thou sleep, O sluggard, and when wilt thou arise out of thy sleep? You rely upon this or that, and 'pretend pretences in sins;' I am waiting for Epiphany; I prefer Easter; I will wait for Pentecost. It is better to be baptized with Christ, to rise with Christ on the Day of His Resurrection, to honour the Manifestation of the Spirit. And what then? The end will come suddenly in a day for which thou lookest not, and in an hour that thou art not aware of; and then you will have for a companion lack of grace.... Therefore do not delay in coming to grace, but hasten, lest the robber outstrip you, lest the adulterer pass you by, lest the insatiate be satisfied before you, lest the murderer seize the blessing first, or the publican or the fornicator, or any of these violent ones who take the Kingdom of heaven by force.[58]

Gregory tenaciously cajoles his listeners and gives *us* additional glimpses of the baptismal customs with which his community was familiar and to which they had become perhaps too attached.

Let us be like Peter and John, and let us hasten; as they did to the Sepulchre and the Resurrection, so we to the Font; running together, racing against each other, striving to be first to obtain this Blessing. And say not, 'Go away, and come again, and to-morrow I will be baptized,' when you may have the blessing today. 'I will have with me father, mother, brothers, wife, children, friends, and all whom I value, and then I will be saved; but it is not yet the fitting time for me to be made bright;' for if you say so, there is reason to fear lest you should have as sharers of your sorrow those whom you hoped to have as sharers of your joy. If they will be with you, well; — but do not wait for them. For it is base to say, 'But where is my offering for my baptism, and where is my baptismal robe, in which I shall be made bright, and where is what is wanted for the entertainment of my baptizers, that in these too I may become worthy of notice? For, as you see, all these things are necessary, and on account of this the Grace will be lessened.' Do not trifle with great things, or allow yourself to think so basely. The Sacrament is greater than the visible environment. Offer *yourself*; clothe yourself with Christ, feast me with your conduct; I rejoice to be thus affectionately treated, and God Who gives these great gifts rejoices thus. Nothing is great in the sight of God, but what the poor may give, so that the poor may not here also be outrun, for they cannot contend with the rich. In other matters there is a distinction between poor and rich, but here the more willing is the richer.[59]

Apparently, some were even measuring baptismal grace bestowed in terms of the bestower's position in church hierarchy or holiness of life, because Gregory continues:

Do not say, "A Bishop shall baptize me, and he a Metropolitan, and he of Jerusalem (for the Grace does not come of a place, but of the Spirit), and he of noble birth, for it would be a sad thing for my nobility to be insulted by being baptized by a man of no family." Do not say, "I do not mind a mere Priest, if he is a celibate, and a religious, and of angelic life; for it would be a sad thing for me to be defiled even in the moment of my cleansing." Do not ask for credentials of the preacher or the baptizer. For another is his judge, and the examiner of what thou canst not see. For man looketh on the outward appearance, but the Lord looketh on the heart. But to thee let every one be trustworthy for purification, so only he is one of those who have been approved, not of those who are openly condemned, and not a stranger to the Church.... And so anyone can be your baptizer; for though one may excel another in his life, yet the grace of baptism is the same, and anyone may be your consecrator who is formed in the same faith.[60]

Gregory's homily on baptism is a treasure trove of information about the baptismal practices and interpretations with which he was familiar. For example, catechumens were not safe from the wiles of the devil. Gregory warns:

Take not thine enemy to be thy counsellor; despise not to be and to be called Faithful. As long as you are a Catechumen you are but in the porch of Religion; you must come inside, and cross the court, and observe the Holy Things, and look into the Holy of Holies, and be in company with the Trinity. Great are the interests for which you are fighting, great too the stability which you need. Protect yourself with the shield of faith. He fears you, if you fight armed with this weapon, and therefore he would strip you the Gift, that he may the more easily overcome you unarmed and defenceless. He assails every age, and every form of life; he must be repelled by all.[61]

Infants were baptized. Gregory says:

Have you an infant child? Do not let sin get any opportunity, but let him be sanctified from his childhood; from his very tenderest age let him be consecrated by the Spirit. Fearest thou the Seal on account of the weakness of nature? O what a small-souled mother, and of how little faith! Why, Anna even before Samuel was born promised him to God, and after his birth consecrated him at once, and brought him up in the priestly habit, not fearing anything in human nature, but trusting in God. You have no need of amulets or incantations, with which the Devil also comes in, stealing worship from God for himself in the minds of vainer men. Give your child the Trinity, that great and noble Guard.[62]

Infant baptism was perfectly acceptable in emergencies, but otherwise Gregory believes it is probably better to wait until children can speak for themselves. He says:

Be it so, some will say, in the case of those who ask for Baptism; what have you to say about those who are still children, and conscious neither of the loss nor of the grace? Are we to baptize them too? Certainly, if any danger presses. For it is better that they should be unconsciously sanctified than that they should depart unsealed and uninitiated. A proof of this is found in the Circumcision on the eighth day, which was a sort of typical seal, and was conferred on children before they had the use of reason. And so is the anointing of the doorposts.... But in respect of others, I give my advice to wait till the end of the third year, or a little more or less, when they may be able to listen and to answer something about the Sacrament; that, even though they do not perfectly understand it, yet at any rate they may know the outlines; and then to sanctify them in soul and body with the great sacrament of our consecration.[63]

Exorcism was a part of the baptismal ritual, to which there was apparently some resistance:

From the day of your new birth all the old marks were effaced, and Christ was put upon all in one form. Do not disdain to confess your sins, knowing how John baptized, that by present shame you may escape from future shame.... Do not reject the medicine of exorcism, nor refuse it because of its length. This too is a touchstone of your right disposition for grace.[64]

Confession of faith in the Trinity was also a part of the rite, as Gregory says:

> Besides all this and before all, keep I pray you the good deposit, by which I live and work, and which I desire to have as the companion of my departure; with which I endure all that is so distressful, and despise all delights; the confession of the Father and the Son and the Holy Ghost. This I commit unto you to-day; with this I will baptize you and make you grow. This I give you to share, and to defend all your life, the One Godhead and Power, found in the Three in Unity, and comprising the Three separately, not unequal, in substances or natures, neither increased nor diminished by superiorities or inferiorities; in every respect equal, in every respect the same; just as the beauty and the greatness of the heavens is one; the infinite conjunction of Three Infinite Ones, Each God when considered in Himself; as the Father so the Son, as the Son so the Holy Ghost; the Three One God when contemplated together; Each God because Consubstantial; One God because of the Monarchia.[65]

Psalmody and the lighting of lamps also accompanied the rite:

> But one thing more I preach unto you. The Station in which you shall presently stand after your Baptism before the Great Sanctuary is a foretype of the future glory. The Psalmody with which you will be received is a prelude to the Psalmody of Heaven; the lamps which you will kindle are a Sacrament of the illumination there with which we shall meet the Bridegroom, shining and virgin souls, with the lamps of our faith shining....[66]

The Feast of Lights homilies give us more information about Cappadocian baptismal practices than did their paschal and Lenten counterparts, but they do not provide any glimpses of baptismal preparation, other than Basil's discussion of Epiphany enrollment. The preachers seem much more concerned to get people into the font lest they die unbaptized than they be properly prepared for baptism.

As for Christmas, our homilies celebrate most if not all of the elements of the birth narratives found in Matthew and Luke. As he did with his Easter sermon, Amphilochius provides us with a beautiful hymn-like homily for the December 25 feast. His *Oration 1 In Natalitia Domini*[67] begins with a poetic praise of the day and of the salvific consequences of the event that it celebrates:

> This spiritual and radiant meadow, which has been embroidered with the beauty of the heavenly flowers and which smells sweet with the apostolic and undefiled

scents, appears to me to be an image of the divine paradise. For just as that scent and pure place is brightened with imperishable trees and immortal fruits and countless other exceedingly bright beauties, indeed so also this most godlike banquet of the most sacred church is made splendid by mental and inexpressible mysteries, of which our unbroken foundation and unshaken foundation stone and saving corner and all-venerable crown is the feast today of the holy birthday of Christ our true God; on account of which both the old things are prophesied typologically and the new things are proclaimed explicitly to the whole inhabited earth, on account of which heaven is opened and earth <is> raised up to divine height, on account of which paradise is given back to humans and the power of death is abolished, on account of which the power of corruption is trampled and deadly worship of the devil is at an end, on account of which human suffering is put to death, the life of absolute angelic rule is renewed, on account of which deceit of demons is driven away, wisdom and all-hallowed coming of God is revealed.[68]

Amphilochius continues, listing some of the elements that comprise the feast's content:

"For the Lord himself," it says, "will come and save us" (Is. 63.9). In what manner do you proclaim that the Lord comes to us, O divine prophet? For I will speak openly to you in this matter, having taken upon myself the face of the old men, who have not celebrated these things in the all-praised festal assembly, nor made proof of the new and all-hallowed birth from the undefiled virgin, nor looked upon the heavenly herald, indeed I mean the most godlike star, nor seen the leaps of the holy angels, nor heard the divine voices which, having rejoiced, they reported to the priestly shepherds, proclaiming the begotten savior, nor understood the gifts of the magi and the divine adoration; having taken up the face of those, I may ask you about the manner of the coming.[69]

He weaves together scriptures from both testaments to illustrate how the birth of Christ fulfilled prophecy and in what a paradoxical manner this occurred.

So how should we glorify the feast today? How should we bless the most mysterious festal gathering for the present? For what will trace out the immortal wealth of this day? With what kind of sublime-sounding and loftiest words should we proclaim this all-praised and mystery of incorruptibility to which trophies are dedicated? O worthy day of countless hymns, in which the star rose out of Jacob (Num. 24.17), and the heavenly human, who appeared out of Israel, and the "mighty God" visited us, and the "sun of righteousness" overshadowed (Mal. 3.20) and the treasury of the divine virtues is opened, and the plant of eternal life sprouted to humans (Zech 6.12), and the dawn from heaven shone forth, and the Master of the heavenly things and earthly things has come out of a maiden's womb into a perishable world for the redemption of the world. "For a savior was born to us today, who is Christ the Lord" (Luke 2.11), who is a "light of the Gentiles" and "salvation of the house of Israel" (Luke 2.32, Is. 42.6). O wonder! The one who is not circumscribed by the heavens encamped in a manger as a young child, and the one who established all things with a little word was comforted by feminine arms, and the one who had freely given being to all the supramundane powers was suckled by the undefiled breasts of the holy virgin.[70]

Amphilochius continues to rhapsodize:

O Bethlehem, consecrated city that is also joined in lot with humans! O manger, o manger partaking with the cherubim and equally honored with the seraphim. For the one who is divinely borne eternally by those thrones, now in turn corporeally finds lodging in you. O Mary, o Mary, she who possesses as firstborn the creator of all things! O humanity, who has corporeally invested with being the eternal word of God and who has been honored above the heavenly and intellectual powers in this matter![71]

Gregory of Nazianzus contrasts the Christian feast with pagan solstice celebrations and customs. He exhorts, "Let us not adorn our porches, nor arrange dances, nor decorate streets; let us not feast the eye, nor enchant the ear with music, nor enervate the nostrils with perfume, nor prostitute the taste, nor indulge the touch, those roads that are so prone to evil and entrances for sin...."[72] He continues:

Let us leave all these to the Greeks and to the pomps and festivals of the Greeks, who call by the name of gods beings who rejoice in the reek of sacrifices, and who consistently worship with their belly; evil inventors and worshippers of evil demons. But we, the Object of whose adoration is the Word, if we must in some way have luxury, let us seek it in word, and in the Divine Law, and in histories; especially such as are the origin of this Feast; that our luxury may be akin to and not far removed from Him Who hath called us together.[73]

Gregory then discourses on the incomprehensibility of the divine nature but calls himself back to the subject at hand, saying, "This, however, is all I must now say about God; for the present is not a suitable time, as my present subject is not the doctrine of God but that of the Incarnation. But when I say God, I mean Father, Son, and Holy Ghost."[74] However, first he briefly discusses what he feels are errors in heretical and Jewish theology, as well as the genesis of heavenly and angelic powers. Then in words very similar to some used in his Easter sermon of 383, he says:

But perhaps some one of those who are too festive and impetuous may say, What has all this to do with us? Spur your horse to the goal. Talk to us about the Festival, and the reasons for our being here to-day. Yes, this is what I am about to do, although I have begun at a somewhat previous point, being compelled to do so by love, and by the needs of my argument.[75]

Finally, Gregory gets to what, for him, is the essence of this feast. He preaches on the creation of the invisible (angelic) and visible worlds, the creation of humans as the mingling of these two worlds, the Fall of Adam and Eve, their banishment from Eden and punishment, and the many chastisements used by God in an attempt to reconcile lost humanity.[76] Then, the Word takes flesh, an event that Gregory praises:

> O new commingling; O strange conjunction; the Self-Existent comes into being, the Uncreate is created, That which cannot be contained is contained, by the intervention of an intellectual soul, mediating between the Deity and the corporeity of the flesh. And He Who gives riches becomes poor, for He assumes the poverty of my flesh, that I may assume the richness of His Godhead.[77]

Gregory of Nyssa also focuses on the mystery of the incarnation and the elements surrounding Christ's birth, as they are described by Matthew and Luke. He states the reason for the feast:

> And the present occasion of the feast is the mystery of the true tabernacle. For in this the human tent is pitched by the one who clothed himself in humanity for our sake.... Joining in the chorus, let us also say that of the psalmody by the lofty David, that "Blessed is the one who comes in the name of the Lord" (Ps. 117.26). How does he come? Not, as it were, by means of some ship or chariot, but having passed through to the human life through the incorruption of a maiden.[78]

As he would do in his Ascension and Pentecost sermons of 388, Gregory uses the psalmody to set the joyful tone of the feast. He also makes use of the feast's coincidence with the winter solstice. He says:

> Come indeed, having stirred up our souls to the spiritual dance, let us choose David as leader and guide and chief of our chorus and let us say with him that sweet sound, which, having anticipated, we sang. And let us take it up again, that "This is the day which the Lord has made, let us rejoice and be glad in it" (Ps. 117.24) in which the darkness begins to decrease and the duration of the night is forcibly compressed to eclipse by the one who exceeds the sunbeam. Brothers, through accident, some such non-accidental plan with respect to the feast has now become the manifestation of the divine life to human life. But the creation fully describes some mystery to the clearer-sighted ones through the things that are visible, all but sending forth sound and teaching the one who is able to hear, what the day being increased and the night being shortened means in the coming of the master. For *I* am determined to hear the creation as it expounds any such things, because when you see these things, O hu-

man, observe the secret being made manifest to you through the things that are visible. Do you see the night having advanced to the greatest length and halting at the high point of movement and returning in the opposite way? Observe that the evil night of sin was also as long, and having increased through every thought of evils and having arrived first at the highest magnitude of wickedness, today has been driven back further than the law, and the things from this are being brought to cessation and also destruction. Do you see the more lasting beam of light and the higher sun of fellowship? Perceive the coming of the true light that illuminates the whole inhabited world with the beams of the gospel.[79]

Like Gregory of Nazianzus, Gregory of Nyssa goes off on tangents, and his calling himself back to the point gives us information about what he thinks the essence of the feast is. After enumerating events from the Hebrew scriptures in which God did not self-manifest in human form and discoursing on the evils of humans and Satan, Gregory says:

But let us return to the present joy which the angels proclaim to the shepherds, which the heavens tell to the magi, which the spirit of prophecy publishes abroad through many and different ones, as also the magi become heralds of the grace.... Do you hear Isaiah crying out, "A child has been born to us, and a son has been given to us" (Is. 9.6)? Learn from the prophet himself how the child was born, how a son was given. According to the law of nature? No, says the prophet, the master of nature is not a slave to the laws of nature. But say how the child has been born. "Look," he says, "the virgin will conceive and will bear a son and will call his name Emmanuel, which means God with us" (Is. 7.14).[80]

After another excursus—this one on the perpetual virginity of Mary—Gregory once again calls himself back to the topics of the day:

But we have wandered far from the things set before [us]; it is necessary to return to the word about Bethlehem in the gospel. For if we really are shepherds and keep a watchful eye on our own flocks, the voice of the angels that is proclaiming this great joy is certainly for us. Accordingly, let us look up into the heavenly army, let us see the chorus of angels, let us hear their divine hymning. What is the sound of those who are keeping festival? They cry aloud "Glory to God in the highest" (Lk. 2.14). For what reason does the voice of the angels glorify the deity who is being beheld in the highest? Because, it says, "And peace on earth." The angels have become very glad because of the one who appears; peace on earth.... Having heard these things let us go into Bethlehem, let us see the new wonder, how the virgin glories in childbirth, how the unwedded one nurses the infant. But first, let us hear who and from where she is from those who record things about her.[81]

Gregory then gives some of Mary's history, which he has learned from "some hidden account" (ἀποκρύφου τινὸς ἱστορίας); he talks about her birth, childhood and youth,[82] and her *initiation* by Gabriel. He says, "Then the virgin is initiated (μυσταγωγεῖται) by Gabriel. And the words of the initiation were a blessing. 'Hail, highly favored one,' he says, 'the Lord is with you'" (Lk. 1.28), [83] and then goes on to discuss the Annunciation.

Then Gregory finally gets to Bethlehem. He discusses the manger, the swaddling clothes, the animals, the Magi and the Holy Innocents.[84] The Magi account gives Gregory the opportunity to criticize Israel. He says:

> But let us look up to the heavenly wonders. For see, not only prophets and angels announce this joy to us, but the heavens also proclaim the glory of the good news through suitable wonders. Christ springs up to us from Judah, just as the apostle says, but the Jew is not illuminated by the one who has sprung up. The Magi [were] strangers to the covenants of the promise and aliens of the blessing of the fathers, but they outrun the Israelite people to the knowledge, both having discovered the heavenly star and not being ignorant of the king in the cave. Those bring presents, these plot. Those worship, these persecute. Those rejoice when they have found the one being sought, these are troubled at the birth of the one that was revealed.[85]

Gregory concludes this sermon with a section linking the Nativity feast to the Pascha,[86] saying in effect, as did John Chrysostom, that there would be no Easter without Christmas. He exhorts:

> And let no one suspect that such a thanksgiving [εὐχαριστίαν] only suits the mystery in relation to the Pascha. For let him consider that the Pascha is the end of the plan. But how would the end have come if the beginning had not led the way? Which is more primal than which? Quite clearly the birth of the plan in relation to the suffering. So also the beautiful things of the Pascha are part of the honors around the birth, and if someone lays down the good deeds of those recorded in the gospels, and if he goes through the wonders during the healings, the nourishment in the midst of difficulties, the return of those who had died from their graves, the improvised tillage of the wine, the flight of the demons, the changing of manifold sufferings into health, the leaps of the lame, the eyes from clay, the divine teachings, the lawgivings, the instruction of the parables on higher things, all these things are a grace of the present day. For this [day] was the first of a series of good things. Accordingly, "Let us exult and rejoice in it" (Ps. 117.24), not fearing the reproach of humans and, as the prophet commands, not being defeated by their contempt, who scoff at the word of the plan as not being suited to assume the nature of a body and through birth to combine the Lord himself with human life.[87]

Honoring the Holy Innocents

In the earliest extant sermon for the December 25 Nativity feast, given by Optatus of Milevis in Numidia, North Africa around 360 and entitled "On the Birthday of the Infants," the preacher says:

> This is the way of the heavens, the truth of the Gospels, the perpetual way of the saints. *I am the way, the truth and the life. Nobody comes to the Father except by me* (Jn. 14:6). If, then, Christ is the heavenly way which He has paved to be endured by the brothers who would follow him, if, revealing a hidden truth, He gave life to those believing in Him, let us who are sealed in the militia of the faithful follow bravely in the footsteps of Christ. If the world hates us, if the secular power persecutes us, already it hated the Lord Himself and by subtle inquiries sought to kill Him. And when he killed the infants in place of Christ he made a crowd of martyrs, but he did not find Christ whom he had badly looked for.[88]

It is interesting to note that, more than two decades later, both Gregory of Nazianzus and Gregory of Nyssa also mention Herod's slaughter of the Innocents in their Nativity feast homilies. Gregory of Nazianzus says:

> One thing connected with the Birth of Christ I would have you hate...the murder of the infants by Herod. Or rather you must venerate this too, the Sacrifice of the same as Christ, slain before the Offering of the New Victim. If He flees into Egypt, joyfully become a companion of His exile. It is a grand thing to share the exile of the persecuted Christ. If He tarry long in Egypt, call Him out of Egypt by a reverent worship of Him there. Travel without fault through every stage and faculty of the Life of Christ. Be purified, be circumcised; strip off the veil which has covered thee from thy birth. After this teach in the Temple, and drive out the sacrilegious traders. Submit to be stoned if need be, for well I wot thou shalt be hidden from those who cast the stones; thou shalt escape even through the midst of them, like God. If thou be brought before Herod, answer not for the most part. He will respect thy silence more than most people's long speeches. If thou be scourged, ask for what they leave out. Taste gall for the taste's sake; drink vinegar; seek for spittings; accept blows, be crowned with thorns, that is, with the hardness of the godly life; put on the purple robe, take the reed in hand, and receive mock worship from those who mock at the truth; lastly, be crucified with Him, and share His Death and Burial gladly, that thou mayest rise with Him, and be glorified with Him and reign with Him.[89]

Gregory of Nyssa devotes much more time to the Holy Innocents. With a long series of questions, he illustrates the diabolical injustice of Herod's decree that all Bethlehemite male children under the age of two be executed (Matt. 2.16). For example, Gregory asks:

> For what reason is that awful injunction dispatched, the evil pebble [of condemnation] against the infants, to snatch the wretched babies, when they have injured what? Having supplied against themselves what reason for death and punishment, having only one charge—the act of having been begotten and having come into light?[90]

Is it possible that in Cappadocia in the 380s there was no separate feast honoring the Holy Innocents? Current scholarly opinion holds that Christians in Jerusalem observed the Feast of the Holy Innocents on May 18 during this period.[91] There is no evidence of such a spring observance in Cappadocia, but we cannot say that this is because the Innocents were consciously honored on or near December 25. In fact, after his lengthy and sometimes graphic treatment (and embellishment) of the story from Matthew, Gregory returns to the real point of the day:

> But let us lead the preaching away from the dirges for the children and let us turn the mind to more cheerful things and better suiting to the feast, even if, outroaring according to the prophecy, Rachel loudly bewails the slaughter of the children (cf. Jer. 38.15; Matt. 2.17). For in a day of feast, just as the wise Solomon says, forgetfulness of evils is fitting (cf. Ecclus. 11.25). But what should be clearer to us than this feast, in which, having dispersed the evil moonless night of the devil, the sun of righteousness (cf. Mal. 3.20) shines forth to nature through our nature itself, in which what had fallen down is woken up, what had been made hostile is led into reconciliation (cf. Ro. 5.10), what had been sold into slavery is brought back, what had fallen from life returns to life, what had been enslaved in captivity is taken up again into the worth of the kingdom, what had been bound with the bonds of death returns unbound to the place of the living? Now in accordance with the prophecy the bronze gates of death are smashed, the iron bars are shattered (cf. Ps. 106.16; Isa. 45.2), by which the human race was formerly confined in the prison of death. Now the gate of righteousness is opened, just as David says (cf. Ps. 117.19). Now the unison sound of those who are celebrating the festival is heard throughout the whole inhabited world.[92]

Interestingly, Basil discusses Matthew's account of the Magi and Herod but stops short of mentioning the murder of the children. Lacking definitive information, all that can be said is that sometimes this part of Matthew's birth narrative was included in Cappadocian Nativity feast preaching along with many other elements of the Matthean and Lucan accounts, although Gregory of Nyssa clearly considered the happier elements to be more suitable to the feast.

The Kalends of January

In a letter to Libanius, who had been one of Basil's teachers in Athens, Gregory of Nyssa disparages the Roman celebration of the new year, saying:

It was a custom with the Romans to celebrate a feast in winter-time, after the custom of their fathers, when the length of days begins to draw out, as the sun climbs to the upper regions of the sky. Now the beginning of the month is esteemed holy, and by this day auguring the character of the whole year, they devote themselves to forecasting lucky accidents, gladness and wealth. What is my object in beginning my letter in this way? Why, I do so because I too kept this feast, having got my present of gold as well as any of them; for then there came into my hands as well as theirs gold, not like that vulgar gold, which potentates treasure and which those that have it give,—that heavy, vile, and soulless possession,—but that which is loftier than all wealth, as Pindar says (Pindar, *Ol.* i.1: ὁ δὲ χρυσός, αἰθόμενον πῦρ ἅτε διαπρέπει νυκτός, μεγαλάνορος ἔξοχα πλούτου.), in the eyes of those that have sense, being the fairest presentation, I mean your letter, and the vast wealth which it contained. For thus it happened; that on that day, as I was going to the metropolis of the Cappadocians, I met an acquaintance, who handed me this present, your letter, as a new year's gift.[93]

On January 1, 400, Asterius also criticized this holiday that had, apparently, lured some members of his congregation away from church. He says:

Yesterday and to-day two feasts, not only unrelated and discordant, but wholly adverse and hostile to each other have been celebrated. One is of the rabble without, gathering, in large sums, the money of mammon, and bringing in its train bargaining, vulgar and mean. The other is of holy and true religion, inculcating acquaintance with God, and the virtue of the purified life. And since many, preferring the luxury and absorption which arise from vanity, have left off going to church, come, let us with a discourse dispel from your souls this foolish and harmful delight, which as a sort of inflammation of the brain, with laughter and jesting, induces death.[94]

Asterius continues to expose the evils of the festival, contrasting it with the major *Christian* feasts with which he was familiar, celebrated "in orderly succession" with the rest of the feasts. He says:

What then are we to call the festival, or the money spent in it? I cannot make out. But tell me, you who have been wearing yourselves out in preparing for it. Give an account of it, as we do of the festivals which are genuine and according to the will of God. We celebrate the birth of Christ, since at this time God manifested himself in the flesh. We celebrate the Feast of Lights (Epiphany), since by the forgiveness of our sins we are led forth from the dark prison of our former life into a life of light and uprightness. Again, on the day of the resurrection we adorn ourselves and march through the streets with joy, because that day reveals to us immortality and the transformation into a higher existence. Thus we keep these feasts and the rest of them in orderly succession. For every human event there is a reason, but that which lacks reasonable explanation and purpose is stuff and nonsense.[95]

It is obvious from these passages from Gregory and Asterius that "good Christians" did not participate in the revels of the new year celebration, and that the only legitimate holidays were those for which a "reasonable explanation" could be given. The first passage quoted from Asterius's sermon also raises an interesting question. He contrasts the pagan feast, which lasted for several days,[96] with a feast of the "holy and true religion, inculcating acquaintance with God, and the virtue of the purified life." What was this feast? According to Datema, it was Epiphany. He maintains that the pagan feast was celebrated over a period of five days, beginning on December 31 and ending on January 4, and that Asterius is contrasting the Christian feast celebrated "today" (that is, January 5) with the final day of the pagan feast, celebrated "yesterday."[97] Asterius is, therefore, preaching at an Epiphany vigil. This is certainly possible, but it is difficult to say for sure, because Asterius devotes the entire sermon to criticizing the pagan feast and does not mention the Christian feast again, nor does he specify to which day of the pagan feast he is referring. He bemoans the amount of money and energy spent on the feast, as well as the exchange of gifts of money, which Datema says happened on the second day of the festival of the Kalends (that is, January 1), but this may be a general criticism of the entire feast. In addition, although Asterius makes several scriptural references, he is not preaching on a particular text, which might have given us a clue. Asterius's contemporary Augustine of Hippo referred to a Christian feast on January 1; his sermon is similarly devoted to enumerating the evils of the pagan celebration. He also does not say what the Christians are feasting, but he does mention that they had just chanted Psalm 106.47—"Save us, O Lord our God: gather us from among the nations: that we may give thanks to Thy holy name."[98] According to John Gunstone, some early sacramentaries, which he does not identify, prescribe fasts, litanies and processions to counteract the pagan reveling. He also notes that some seventh and eighth-century Roman sources, including the Gelasian Sacramentary, list January 1 as the commemoration of the birth of Mary; as the Octave of Christmas, the day later became the Feast of the Circumcision.[99] In fact, Caesarius of Arles (470–543) informs us that, in his community at least, the day already commemorated that event by the early sixth century.[100] It is also possible that Amaseia was commemorating a martyr, or perhaps Basil of Caesarea, on that day, but that is speculation. Without further information, we cannot identify the feast for sure.

Doctrinal Debates and the Institution of Christmas

Bernard Botte, in his study of the origins of Christmas and Epiphany, was one of the first to observe that both feasts developed in the context of doctrinal controversy in both East and West and that they were used by many pro-Nicene preachers and writers to promote Nicene theology and christology. He writes:

> The two feasts of which we are speaking were developed during the centuries that saw the great theological and christological controversies unfold. They were not created with the intention of controversy, but it is undeniable that they served to instill the orthodox faith, the belief in the dogma of Nicea, Ephesus and Chalcedon.[101]

Other scholars have built on and nuanced Botte's idea; Susan Roll provides a thorough and useful summary and critique of these works.[102] She begins by noting:

> A number of liturgical historians remark in their treatment of the early history of the Christmas feast that it cannot be coincidental that Christmas emerged from the post-Nicaea atmosphere of bitter rivalry between the Nicene and the Arian parties, including the struggles of the mainline church with several such doctrinal and organizational sub-groups. Also relevant were the fact that Christmas spread so quickly when the church was highly localized in nature, and that it was almost forcibly instituted in the East when a very similar Epiphany feast had already been celebrated for some time. Very few secondary sources on the liturgical year however go on to cite comprehensive primary evidence that Christmas was indeed deliberately promoted, not to say instituted, in response to these groups as a perceived threat to unity and consistency in the Christian church.[103]

Roll then discusses this primary evidence, including that provided by our Cappadocian leaders, but does not quote the texts themselves. Such quotation is useful, because these texts show clearly that our preachers did, in fact, seize the opportunity provided by these occasions to draw the battle lines. Basil, for example, laments:

> Oh this improper and evil arrogance! Magi worship, and Christians debate, how God [is] in flesh and in what sort of flesh; and if the human that has been appropriated is perfect or imperfect. May the unnecessary things be silenced in the Church of God; may the true things be glorified; may the things that are silenced not be inves-

tigated. Join yourself to those who welcome the Lord from the heavens with joy. Consider shepherds being instructed, priests interpreting, women making merry, when Mary was taught to rejoice by Gabriel, when Elizabeth had John leaping in the womb over them. Anna proclaimed good news, Simeon took [him] in his arms, worshiping the great God in a small infant; not despising the one who appears, but doxologizing the greatness of his divinity. For the divine power shone through the human body just as light through glass plates, shining through to those who have eyes of the heart that have been made clean, with which we should also be found reflecting the glory of the Lord with a veiled face, in order that we ourselves might be changed from glory into glory, by grace and lovingkindness of our Lord Jesus Christ, to whom [be] glory and power for ever and ever. Amen.[104]

Gregory of Nazianzus provides many examples of this strategy. In his Theophany sermon, he asks, "To this what have those cavillers to say, those bitter reasoners about the Godhead, those detractors of all that is praiseworthy, those darkeners of light, uncultured in respect of wisdom, for whom Christ died in vain, those unthankful creatures, the work of the Evil One?"[105] He goes on to explain:

He was sent, but as man, for He was of a twofold Nature; for He was wearied, and hungered, and was thirsty, and was in an agony, and shed tears, according to the nature of a corporeal being. And if the expression be also used of Him as God, the meaning is that the Father's good pleasure is to be considered a Mission, for to this He refers all that concerns Himself; both that He may honour the Eternal Principle, and because He will not be taken to be an antagonistic God. And whereas it is written both that He was betrayed, and also that He gave Himself up and that He was raised up by the Father, and taken up into heaven; and on the other hand, that He raised Himself and *went* up; the former statement of each pair refers to the good pleasure of the Father, the latter to His own Power. Are you then to be allowed to dwell upon all that humiliates Him, while passing over all that exalts Him, and to count on your side the fact that He suffered, but to leave out of the account the fact that it was of His own will? See what even now the Word has to suffer. By one set He is honoured as God, but is confused with the Father, by another He is dishonoured as mere flesh and severed from the Godhead.[106]

In his homily for the Feast of Lights, Gregory admits to using the tactic of repetition:

Let none be astonished if what I have to say contains some things that I have said before; for not only will I utter the same words, but I shall speak of the same subjects, trembling both in tongue and mind and thought when I speak of God for you too, that you may share this laudable and blessed feeling. And when I speak of God you must be illumined at once by one flash of light and by three. Three in Individualities or Hypostases, if any prefer so to call them, or persons, for we will not quarrel about names so long as the syllables amount to the same meaning; but One in respect of the Substance – that is, the Godhead. For they are divided without division, if I may so say; and they are united in division. For the Godhead is one in three, and the three are one, in whom the Godhead is, or to speak more accurately, Who are the Godhead. Excesses and defects we will omit, neither making the Unity a confusion, nor the division a separation. We would keep equally far from the confusion of Sabellius and from the division of Arius, which are evils diametrically opposed, yet equal in their wickedness. For what need is there heretically to fuse God together, or to cut Him up into inequality?[107]

Then, in his homily on baptism the following day, he says:

But if you still halt and will not receive the perfectness of the Godhead, go and look for someone else to baptize – or rather to drown you: I have not time to cut the Godhead, and to make you dead in the moment of your regeneration, that you should have neither the Gift nor the Hope of Grace, but should in so short a time make shipwreck of your salvation. For whatever you may subtract from the Deity of the Three, you will have overthrown the whole, and destroyed your own being made perfect.[108]

Gregory of Nyssa, in his Feast of Lights homily, extends the criticism to those who deny the divinity of the Holy Spirit:

It may be thou art offended, thou who contendest boldly against the glory of the Spirit, and that thou grudgest to the Spirit that veneration wherewith He is reverenced by the godly. Leave off contending with me: resist, if thou canst, those words of the Lord which gave to men the rule of the Baptismal invocation. What says the Lord's command? 'Baptizing them in the Name of the Father and of the Son and of the Holy Ghost.' How in the Name of the Father? Because He is the primal cause of all things. How in the Name of the Son ? Because He is the Maker of the Creation. How in the Name of the Holy Ghost? Because He is the power perfecting all." "Why then dost thou divide the Three Persons into fragments of different natures, and make Three Gods, unlike one to another, whilst from all thou does receive one and the same grace?[109]

Clearly, the Cappadocians did use the feasts celebrating Christ's incarnation to promote their own doctrines and to refute those of their opponents. However, as Roll points out, this does not necessarily mean that the December 25 feast was deliberately adopted for this purpose. She writes:

In Gregory's Christmas Sermon 38 the total economy of salvation, centered on the Paschal mystery but here approached from the idea of incarnation, provides a setting to score direct hits on certain controverted points of Arian doctrine, though this fact alone need not be taken as *prima facie* proof that Christmas was consciously introduced or promoted with an eye to using it as a rhetorical vehicle.[110]

It should also be noted that the incarnation feasts were not the only occasions that they used for this purpose. We have already seen that Pentecost homilies were used to similar ends; in Chapter Four we will see that the celebrations of saints' days provided additional polemical opportunities.

Notes

1. There are some exceptions, of course. For example, in Egypt the feast of the Epiphany was not originally a nativity feast at all; only in the late fourth century did Egyptian Christians begin to celebrate Christ's birth on January 6.

2. A discussion of the two leading hypotheses for the origin of Christmas is beyond the scope of this paper, as we are not interested in its origins but in its adoption in Cappadocia. For a more information on the "History of Religions" and "Calculation" or "Computational" hypotheses, see Talley, *Origins*, 87–99; Roll, 87–105; 127–163; J. Neil Alexander, *Waiting For the Coming: The Liturgical Meaning of Advent, Christmas, Epiphany* (Washington, D.C.: The Pastoral Press), 44–57.

3. Clement of Alexandria, *Stromata* I.21.146. See Talley, *Origins*, 118–121; Roland H. Bainton, "The Origins of Epiphany," in *Early and Medieval Christianity: The Collected Papers in Church History*, Series One (Boston: Beacon Press, 1962), 22–38.

4. Ammianus Marcellinus, *Rerum gestarum* XXI.2.5, cited in Botte, 46: *Et ut haec die quam celebrantes mense Januario Christiani Epiphania dictitant, progressus in eorum ecclesiam, solemniter numine adorato discessit.*

5. John Chrysostom, *On the Birthday of our Lord Jesus Christ* 1, Carroll and Halton, 162.

6. In *Oration 39 On the Holy Lights*, Gregory says, "At His birth we duly kept Festival, both I, the leader (ἔξαρχος) of the Feast, and you, and all that is in the world and above the world" (*Or.* 39.14, *NPNF*, Series 2, vol. 7, 357). There is some debate about the date of this sermon and its companions (*Orations* 38 and 40). Claudio Moreschini and Paul Gallay (*Grégoire de Nazianze Discours 38–40*, Sources chrétiennes 358 [Paris: Les Éditions du Cerf], 153–159) and Ruether (179) date them to December 25, 379, January 6 and 7, 380. Bernardi (204) and Talley (*Origins*, 137) date them to December 25, 380, January 6 and 7, 381. Justin Mossay (212) does not make a choice ("La Noël et l'Épiphanie en Cappadoce au IVᵉ Siècle," in *Noël-Épiphanie Retour du Christ*, Lex Orandi 40 [Paris : Les Éditions du Cerf, 1967], 212) ; subsequent references to this work will be cited as "La Noël et l'Épiphanie." Gregory was Bishop of Constantinople for several months in 381, but at the request of the Nicene community there, including the new emperor, Theodosius, he had been in the imperial city and preaching since 379 (Ruether, 42–48).

7. Botte, *Origines*, 27–28: *Nous possédons de S. Grégoire de Nazianze deux homélies, l'une sure de Noël, l'autre sur l'Épiphanie, prêchées à Constantinople. Lors de son court passage dans cette Église, il y célébra donc les deux fêtes. Mais celle de Noël est d'institution récente et Grégoire se nomme lui-même l' ἔξαρχος de cette fête (PG 36, 340, dans le sermon sur la fête des Lumières). C'est lui qui l'a instituée et il est intérressant de remarquer que cette innovation n'est pas san relation avec la*

réaction anti-arienne, de même qu'à Alexandrie elle coïncidera avec le mouvement anti-nestorien. See also Cullmann, 30; Mossay, "La Noël et l'Épiphanie," 212. Roll (192) also identifies as part of this group Usener, 261–262, 269; Hans Lietzmann, *Geschichte der alten Kirche* (Berlin: De Gruyter, 1938), 322–323; Pietro Borella, "Appunti sul Natale e l'Epifania a Milano al tempo di S. Ambrogio," in *Mélanges offerts à Dom Bernard Botte* (Louvain: Mont César/Keizersberg Abbey, 1972), 54–55.

8.   McArthur, 47; Evangelos Theodorou, "Saint Jean Chrysostome et la fête de Noël," in Botte, *et al.*, eds., *Noël-Épiphanie*, 206; Talley, *Origins*, 137–138.

9.   Roll, 192.

10. Talley, *Origins*, 138. In his essay "Constantine and Christmas," published in 2000, Talley more clearly accepts the majority opinion that ἔξαρχος means "founder" (Talley, "Constantine and Christmas," in in *Between Memory and Hope: Readings on the Liturgical Year*, ed. Maxwell E. Johnson [Collegeville, MN: The Liturgical Press, 2000], 271). Valens died at Adrianople August 9, 378.

11. Talley, *Origins*, 138.

12. Earlier scholars doubted that Basil wrote this sermon; Usener (249–250) summarizes the reasons and dismisses the conclusion.

13. Fedwick, 9, n. 34.

14. Botte, *Origines*, 29; Talley, *Origins*, 138. Roll (190, n. 71) notes the difference of opinion but does not offer an opinion of her own. Bernardi does not discuss this sermon at all, apparently accepting the arguments against its authenticity.

15. Basil, *In sanctam Christi generationem* 1.

16. Ibid.

17. Ibid. 6.

18. Mossay, "La Noël et l'Épiphanie," 214–215: *Au moment où la Noël prend les noms de Théophanie ou de Nativité, c'est-à-dire vers 380, le terme Épiphanie désignant la fête du 6 janvier, est supplanté par l'expression fête des Lumières* (B.Botte, *Les origines...*, pp. 78–80; Christine Mohrmann, «Épiphanie...», p. 655; E. Pax, art. «Épiphanie»..., col. 875.).

19. Talley, *Origins*, 138.

20. Basil of Caesarea, Letter CCXXXII, *NPNF*, Series 2, vol. 8, 272.

21. F. Loofs, *Eustathius von Sebaste und die Chronologie der Basilius-Briefe: Eine patristische Studie* (Halle, Germany: Niemeyer, 1898), 8 n. 3.

22. Datema, *Amphilochius*, xii.

23. Basil of Caesarea, Letter CCXXXII, *NPNF*, Series 2, vol. 8, 273.

24. The editors of the *NPNF* volume note that this word (λαμπήνη) actually means "covered carriage," but the context dictates that Basil really meant "lamps" (*NPNF*, Series 2, vol. 8, 273, n. 1.

25. Gregory of Nyssa, Letter I, *NPNF*, Series 2, vol. 5., 527. (Letter IV, *GNO*, vol. 8, part 2, 27–30.)

26. Gregory of Nyssa, *On the Making of Man*, *NPNF*, Series 2, vol. 5, 387.

27. Letters 115 and 121.

28. Bernardi, 68; Fedwick, 9, n. 33.

29. Gregory of Nazianzus, *Or.* 43.52.

30. Ruether, 179.

31. Gregory of Nazianzus, *Oration 38 On the Theophany, or Birthday of Christ* 1, *NPNF*, Series 2, vol. 7, 345.
32. Ibid. 3–4, *NPNF*, 345.
33. Ibid. 16, *NPNF*, 350.
34. Ibid. 17, *NPNF*, 350–351.
35. Ruether (179) dates this sermon to 380.
36. Gregory of Nazianzus, *Oration 39 On the Holy Lights* 14, *NPNF*, Series 2, vol. 7, 357.
37. Daniélou, "Chronologie," 372.
38. Gregory of Nyssa, *On the Baptism of Christ: A Sermon for the Day of Lights* 3, *NPNF*, Series 2, vol. 5, 518 (paragraph numbers supplied).
39. Daniélou, "Chronologie," 372.
40. Gregory of Nyssa, *On Saint Stephen* I, *GNO* 10.1.2, 75.4–12, trans. Richard (Casimir) McCambly, available from *The Gregory of Nyssa Homepage* at http://www.bhsu.edu/artssciences/asfaculty/dsalomon/nyssa/home.html; subsequent McCambly translations will be cited by homily and paragraph number as *GNH*.
41. Daniélou, "Chronologie," 372.
42. Asterius of Amaseia, *Laudatio S. protomartyris Stephani* 1.1–2.
43. A homily for Epiphany formerly attributed to Gregory Thaumaturgus has been proven inauthentic (Botte, *Origines*, 26).
44. Basil of Caesarea, *Exhortatoria ad sanctum baptisma* 1.
45. See p. 32.
46. Basil of Caesarea, *Exhortatoria ad sanctum baptisma* 1.
47. Ibid. 7.
48. Gregory of Nazianzus, *Or. 39*.1, *NPNF*, Series 2, vol.7, 352.
49. Ibid. 20, *NPNF*, 359.
50. Gregory of Nazianzus, *Or. 40*.1, *NPNF*, 360.
51. Gregory of Nyssa, *On the Baptism of Christ* 2, *NPNF*, Series 2, vol. 5, 518.
52. Ibid. 3, *NPNF*, 518. See passage cited above, p. 68.
53. Gregory of Nazianzus *Or. 40*.11, *NPNF*, Series 2, vol. 7, 363.
54. Gregory of Nyssa, *On the Baptism of Christ* 2, *NPNF*, Series 2, vol. 5, 518.
55. Ibid. 3, *NPNF*, 519.
56. Ibid. 4, NPNF, 520.
57. Gregory of Nazianzus, *Or. 40*.13, *NPNF*, Series 2, vol. 7, 364.
58. Ibid. 24, *NPNF*, 368.
59. Ibid. 25, *NPNF*, 368–369.
60. Ibid. 26, *NPNF*, 369.
61. Ibid. 16, *NPNF*, 365.
62. Ibid. 17, *NPNF*, 365.
63. Ibid. 28, *NPNF*, 370.
64. Ibid. 27, *NPNF*, 369.
65. Ibid. 41, *NPNF*, 375.
66. Ibid. 46, *NPNF*, 377.
67. The Greek title, translated "On the Birthday Feast of Our Great God and Savior Jesus Christ," uses the term τὰ γενέθλια for this feast.
68. Amphilochius of Iconium, *In Natalitia* 1.

69. Ibid.

70. Ibid. 3.

71. Ibid. 4.

72. Gregory of Nazianzus, *Or.* 38.5, *NPNF*, Series 2, vol. 7, 346.

73. Ibid. 6, *NPNF*, 346.

74. Ibid. 8, *NPNF*, 347.

75. Ibid. 10, *NPNF*, 348.

76. Ibid. 11–13.

77. Ibid. 13, *NPNF*, 349.

78. Gregory of Nyssa, *In diem natalem salvatoris* 2. Daniélou dates this sermon to December 25, 386 (Daniélou, "Chronologie," 372).

79. Ibid. 4.

80. Ibid. 7.

81. Ibid. 10.

82. Ibid. 11.

83. Ibid. 12.

84. Ibid. 13–15.

85. Ibid. 14.

86. John Chrysostom makes a similar statement in his homily on the anniversary of Philogonius of Antioch, five days before Christmas (PG 48.703).

87. Gregory of Nyssa, *In diem natalem salvatoris* 17.

88. Optatus of Milevis, *On the Birthday of the Infants* 3; Carroll and Halton, 150.

89. Gregory of Nazianzus *Or.* 38.18, *NPNF*, Series 2, vol. 7, 351.

90. Gregory of Nyssa, *In diem natalem salvatoris* 14.

91. John F. Baldovin, *The Urban Character of Christian Worship: The Origins, Development, and Meaning of Stational Liturgy*, Orientalia Christiana Analecta, ed. Robert F. Taft, no. 228 (Rome: Pont. Institutum Studiorum Orientalium, 1987), 87–90; J. Neil Alexander, "Principal Aspects of Sacred Time in Byzantine Jerusalem," (Th.D. diss., The General Theological Seminary, 1993), 87–90.

92. Gregory of Nyssa, *In diem natalem salvatoris* 16.

93. Gregory of Nyssa, Letter XI, *NPNF* Series 2, vol. 5, 533–534. (Letter XIV, *GNO*, vol. 8, part 2, 46–48.)

94. Asterius of Amaseia, *On the Festival of the Calends* 1, *Ancient Sermons for Modern Times by Asterius, Bishop of Amasia*, trans. Galusha Anderson and Edgar Johnson Goodspeed (New York: Pilgrim Press, 1904), 113–114. Paragraph numbers are supplied to correspond to Datema text. Subsequent references to this volume of translations will be cited as *Ancient Sermons*.

95. Ibid. 3, 115–117.

96. Mossay notes that the January revels were very popular feasts in the fourth century, particularly in the eastern half of the empire. He also says that, according to Libanius, the activities for January 1 through 3 included taking of vows of loyalty to the state and the emperor, as well as exchanging gifts, banqueting and dancing ("La Noël et l'Épiphanie," 228–229).

97. Datema, *Asterius*, 228–229.

98. Augustine, Sermon 198 *On 1 January, Against the Pagans* 1, *The Works of Saint Augustine: Translation for the 21ˢᵗ Century*, vol. 3, *Sermons*, part 6, On the Liturgi-

cal Seasons, trans. Edmund Hill, ed. John E. Rotelle (New Rochelle, NY: New City Press, 1993), 73.

99. John Gunstone, *Christmas and Epiphany* (London: The Faith Press, 1967), 74–75.
100. Carroll and Halton, 191.
101. Botte, *Origines*, 86: *Les deux fêtes dont nous parlons se sont développées au cours des siècles qui ont vu se dérouler les grandes controverses théologiques et christologiques. Elles n'ont pas été créées dans un but de controverse; mais il est indéniable qu'elles ont servie à faire pénétrer la foi orthodoxe, la croyance au dogme de Nicée, d'Éphèse et de Chalcédoine.*
102. Roll, 183–189.
103. Ibid. 165.
104. Basil, In *sanctam Christi generationem* 6.
105. Gregory of Nazianzus, *Or.* 38.14, *NPNF*, Series 2, vol. 7, 349.
106. Ibid. 15, *NPNF*, 350.
107. Gregory of Nazianzus, *Or.* 39.11, *NPNF*, 355–356.
108. Gregory of Nazianzus, *Or.* 40.44, *NPNF*, 376.
109. Gregory of Nyssa, *On the Baptism of Christ* 4, *NPNF*, Series 2, vol. 5, 520.
110. Roll, 191.

Chapter 4

The Sanctoral Cycle

By the time Asterius was Bishop of Amaseia in the late fourth and early fifth centuries, the celebration of saints' feast days was a deeply entrenched and beloved practice. In his *Encomium on the Holy Martyrs*, he writes:

> For if the devil had not persecuted Christians and stirred up the battle against the church, we would not have martyrs; but when martyrs did not exist, our life was gloomy and festival-less. For what is worth as much as these festal gatherings? And what is so venerable and all-good as seeing the whole city constantly going out of town with the whole population, and attaining the holy place of truest godliness to accomplish the pure mysteries? But true godliness is to worship God and also to honor those who have staunchly borne sufferings for his sake and have stood ready to the last danger of death, of whom the leaders and chiefs who lead the people meet us here today; men who are immortal on account of a good death, who live always because of the scorning of life, who have taken the kingdom in exchange for the blood and have shown forth the treacherous flesh as benefactor of the soul.[1]

Gregory of Nyssa attributes the establishment—or at least a great deal of enrichment—of the cycle of such festal gatherings to another of Pontus's bishops, Gregory Thaumaturgus, Bishop of Neocaesarea in the middle of the third century, including the period of the Decian persecution (250–251). Describing his activities when the persecution came to an end, Gregory of Nyssa writes:

> When that tyranny had been broken by God's help and peace again made room for the human life in which it was easy for all to devote themselves to the divine in freedom, and when he had descended again to the city and visited the whole countryside round about, he gave [953B H53] to peoples everywhere an increase of devotion toward the divine by decreeing festivals in honor of those who had borne up bravely for the faith. Taking up the bodies of the martyrs here and there, gathering together on the anniversary by the yearly cycle, they rejoiced as they kept festival in honor of the martyrs.[2]

As was the case with the paschal and incarnation constellations of that yearly cycle, it is impossible to say exactly what the Cappadocian sanctoral constellation looked like. However, much information on this topic does survive from our group of preachers, and this chapter will organize and analyze the data in an attempt to present as full a picture as possible.

Reconstructing the Cycle

We are able to establish with certainty that Caesarea observed the feast of St. Eupsychius on September 7 and that Basil convened a yearly synod in Eupsychius's honor to which his suffragan bishops were invited, as well as others, including Amphilochius of Iconium, Eusebius of Samosata and the bishops of Pontus. According to Sozomen, Eupsychius was a Caesarean noble and newlywed who was martyred during the reign of Julian (332–364) for his role in the destruction of the Temple of the goddess Τύχη (Fortuna) in that city.[3] In the summer of 372, Basil wrote to Eusebius:

> If it be possible, I beg that this meeting between us may take place at the Synod which we hold every year, in memory of the blessed martyr Eupsychius, now about to be held on the 7th of September. I am compassed with anxieties which demand your help and sympathy, both in the matter of the appointment of bishops and in the consideration of the trouble caused me by the simplicity of Gregory of Nyssa, who is summoning a Synod at Ancyra and leaving nothing undone to counteract me.[4]

The following year he wrote to an Accountant of the Prefects, of which there were two in every province, "I assembled all my brethren the chorepiscopi at the synod of the blessed martyr Eupsychius to introduce them to your excellency. On account of your absence they must be brought before you by letter."[5] In 374, Basil invited Amphilochius, although he seems to have gotten the date wrong. He writes to his friend:

> God grant that when this letter is put into your hands, it may find you in good health, quite at leisure, and as you would wish to be. For then it will not be in vain that I send you this invitation to be present at our city to add greater dignity to the annual festival which it is the custom of our Church to hold in honour of the martyrs. For be sure my most honoured and dear friend, that our people here, though they have had experience of many, desire no one's presence so eagerly as they do yours; so affectionate an impression has your short intercourse with them left behind. So, then, that the Lord may be glorified, the people delighted, the martryrs honoured, and that I in my old age may receive the attention due to me from my true son, do not refuse to travel to me with all speed. I will beg you too to anticipate the day of assembly, that so we may converse at leisure and may comfort one another by the interchange of spiritual gifts. The day is the fifth of September. Come then three days before hand in order that you may also honour with your presence the Church of the Hospital.[6]

Basil's invitation of 376 to the bishops of Pontus also survives, and from it we gather that the other martyrs to whom he refers in the letter to Amphilochius are Damas and Eupsychius's other unnamed temple-destroying companions. The letter also indicates that these bishops had not attended this synod in a while. Basil writes:

> The honours of martyrs ought to be very eagerly coveted by all who rest their hopes on the Lord, and more especially by you who seek after virtue. By your disposition towards the great and good among your fellow servants you are shewing your affection to our common Lord. Moreover, a special reason for this is to be found in the tie, as it were, of blood, which binds the life of exact discipline to those who have been made perfect through endurance. Since then Eupsychius and Damas and their company are most illustrious among martyrs, and their memory is yearly kept in our city and all the neighbourhood, the Church, calling on you by my voice, reminds you to keep up your ancient custom of paying a visit. A great and good work lies before you among the people, who desire to be edified by you, and are anxious for the reward dependent on the honour paid to the martyrs. Receive, therefore, my supplications, and consent of your kindess to give at cost of small trouble to yourselves a great boon to me.[7]

The SM and HM do not list any commemorations for this region for September 7, nor, oddly, does the HM refer anywhere to a commemoration of Eupsychius.[8] The SM does list a commemoration of Eupsychius and others on January 22.[9] The *Typikon* lists September 7 as the feast of Eupsychius.[10]

Another September feast day was that of St. Mamas, a shepherd who was martyred in Cappadocia in the late third century. In his sermon honoring Mamas, Basil identifies the day; he says:

> May the one who has brought this festal gathering of ours around, having brought last year's prayers to an end and having given a starting point to the following season (for this day designates to us the past cycle and, in turn, becomes the starting point for the approaching one), therefore may the one who has gathered together and who forgives the action of the future carefully guard us in him unharmed, unmolested, not snatched away by the wolf....[11]

It is the first day of the new year. In Basil's time, the civil new year was probably still observed on September 23 in Asia Minor.[12] Apparently, however, Mamas was also honored in the spring in parts of Cappadocia. Gregory of Nazianzus preached his homily *In novam Dominicam* on the Sunday after Easter, April 16, 383, according to Bernardi,[13] and in this homily he refers to the drawing power (and shepherding ability) of St. Mamas, who was "herding people out of the capital city and today renewing the spring to the many thousands of those being driven from every direction."[14] Apparently, this alternate feast day was observed near Caesarea; Bernardi suggests that Mamas's tomb was located just outside the city to the northeast.[15]

In a letter to Theodore of Tyana, Gregory of Nazianzus gives us the exact date of another Cappadocian feast day, although he does not specify the saints being honored. Requesting rather forcefully that Theodore come for a visit, Gregory writes:

> You owe me, even as a sick man, tending, for one of the commandments is the visitation of the sick. And you also owe to the Holy Martyrs their annual honour, which we celebrate in your own Arianzus on the 23rd of the month which we call Dathusa. And at the same time there are ecclesiastical affairs not a few which need our common examination. For all these reasons then, I beg you to come at once: for though the labour is great, the reward is equivalent.[16]

A note in the *NPNF* translation states that Dathusa corresponds to July. This is incorrect. Dathusa corresponded roughly with September, and 23 Dathusa would be September 30. However, the translation of the letter is also incorrect. The Greek text actually gives the date of 22 Dathusa, which is the equivalent of September 29. It is difficult to say whether this was a feast of *all* the martyrs or of particular martyrs. The SM lists the commemoration in Perinthus in Thrace of a bishop named Eutyches and the martyrs Genesius, Sabinus and Eutyches on September 29, and the *Typikon* lists Cyriacus the Anchorite, the martyrs of Palestine, Truphon, Trophimus, Dorymedon, Petronia and Anastasia.[17]

In the oration on Basil given by Gregory of Nazianzus, Gregory talks about the acrimony caused by Valens's division of Cappadocia and mentions a chapel dedicated to St. Orestes, who lived in Tyana and was martyred during the Diocletian persecution. This memorial chapel had become yet another source of tension between Basil and Anthimus of Tyana; according to Gregory, Anthimus was peeved because the revenues of the churches of the Taurus, including the offerings from the chapel of St. Orestes, were going to Caesarea, not Tyana.[18] Delehaye notes that the account of Orestes's martyrdom mentions such a mountain tomb. He writes, "The church of Tyana in Cappadocia was brought fame by the martyrdom of Saint Orestes. The Passion relates that his body, thrown into the waves, was collected by the faithful and buried on the mountain next to the city, where he continued to cure the sick."[19] The fact that a chapel existed in Basil's day indicates that Orestes must have been on the sanctoral calendar, but we do not have any information about his feast day. The HM indicates that Orestes was honored in Alexandria and Constantinople on July 3, although he is not included in a list of martyrs commemorated in Cappadocia on that day.[20]

We can also establish with a fair degree of certainty that St. Stephen the Protomartyr was commemorated by Cappadocians on the day after Christmas, once that feast was established in this region. We noted in Chapter 2 that both Gregory of Nyssa and Asterius of Amaseia place the feast of Stephen in relation to the Nativity feast. Gregory says, "Yesterday the Lord of the universe welcomed us whereas today it is the imitator of the Lord." [21] Asterius says, "So then yesterday we learned through the cyclical and customary feast that the Savior of the world was born.... But today we see the noble combatant being stoned to death for his sake, in order that he might repay with blood the grace for the sake of blood."[22] What is difficult to say from these texts is whether the saint's feast existed in Cappadocia prior to the adoption of the December 25 Nativity feast. It is interesting to note, however, that Stephen's cult existed here before the discovery of his remains near Jerusalem in 415.[23]

Gregory's second homily on St. Stephen also gives us a clue about other saints' commemorations that may have taken place during that time of year. Apparently, Gregory did not have the energy to finish his sermon on Stephen's actual feast day and, therefore, decided to continue the next day. He apologizes to his congregation but notes that the honoring of saints cannot be restricted to just their feast days and adds, "Today we wish to make memory of him along with the holy Apostles."[24] Does this mean that the day following the feast of Stephen was a feast honoring the apostles, at least in Nyssa? It is possible. A little later in the sermon, Gregory makes a comment that suggests that it was the day set aside for commemorating at least three of them, urging celebratory remembrance of Peter, James and John and, indeed, of all the apostles.[25] There is another tantalizing remark in Gregory's sermon in posthumous praise of Basil. In attempting to convince his listeners of Basil's worthiness to be honored on the anniversary of his death, January 1, Gregory talks about an "order of spiritual feasts" ordained by the apostles, especially Paul, which consisted in "having a knowledge of heavenly reality." Gregory says, "The order of yearly celebrations concurs with this apostolic sequence" except that now the feast celebrating "the Only-Begotten

Son's theophany through his birth from a virgin" has been instituted as the "feast of feasts." Then he says:

> Therefore let us number those who follow this order which for us begins with the assembly of apostles and prophets. Indeed people like Stephen, Peter, James, John and Paul possess the apostolic and prophetic spirit after whom comes the pastor and teacher [didaskalos, Basil] who belongs to their order which marks our present cele-bration. What, then, is this festival? Shall I speak of the name or the grace which suffices to reveal the man instead of the name? You know that there is a teacher and shepherd among the Apostles and comprehend the meaning of such titles. I am speaking about Basil....[26]

If this really is the sequence of the yearly cycle with which Gregory was familiar, it supports the hypothesis that Peter, James and John (and perhaps Paul) were honored during the days after the feast of Stephen, and also sug-gests that Gregory considered the Theophany/Nativity feast to be the begin-ning of that cycle, at least metaphorically. The SM contains a similar arrangement, although not specifically for Cappadocia, with Stephen on De-cember 26, John and James on the 27th, Paul and Peter on the 28th.[27] The HM begins on December 25 with the celebration of the birth of Christ, among a great many other commemorations, including the feast of St. Anastasia in Constantinople.[28] For December 26 it lists, among others, the commemora-tion of Stephen, although it also lists Stephen's feast in Rome on December 30.[29] December 27 is reserved exclusively for the commemoration of James, the brother of our Lord, first bishop of Jerusalem and martyr, and of the as-sumption near Ephesus of John the Evangelist.[30] Interestingly, the Holy In-nocents, among many others, including Thomas, are listed for December 28,[31] and Paul is listed for December 30.[32] In the *Typikon*, Stephen is com-memorated on December 27 and the Holy Innocents on the 29th; John, James, Peter and Paul have been moved to other months.[33]

Gregory of Nyssa also provides hints about the time of year during which the feast of the Forty Martyrs of Sebaste occurred. These men were soldiers of the empire under the Emperor Licinius and in the winter or early spring of 320 were stationed in Sebaste in Armenia Minor. Licinius ordered the troops to make sacrifices to the gods, but, as Christians, these soldiers re-fused. They were warned, threatened, whipped and jailed but still refused to make the sacrifice. Finally, they were stripped and placed on a frozen pond, where they were slowly frozen to death and then their bodies burned (al-though, as we shall see, Christians somehow managed to spirit away a good number of their relics). In one of his homilies for the day on which these martyrs were honored, delivered in Ibora, near their resting place,[34] Gregory indicates that their feast day occurred at the beginning of Lent. He says, "This was the time; these [are] the days of the struggle; this is the opening of the Pascha, the mystery of the holy period of forty days. The forty days of propitiation for you and the crowns of the struggles are equal in number."[35] In another sermon given a few days later on the same topic, he says:

> I have said these things in order that we might be persuaded that the martyrs are living, and they are bodyguards and coadjutors of God, who today have assisted and adorned our church; but this fortieth is more radiant and greater, having the remembrance of the 40 martyrs...and the miserable winter no longer seems severe to me; nor do I angrily complain against the savageness of the present season.[36]

Basil also preached a homily on these martyrs, but he does not give us information that would help us establish their feast date. The SM does not list the Forty Martyrs of Sebaste, but the HM places their feast on March 9, as does the *Typikon*.[37]

Another of Basil's extant eulogies for a martyr was composed for the feast of St. Gordius, which is not included in the SM or the HM but is listed as January 3 in the *Typikon*.[38] Basil does not indicate the date, but he does say, "Who is the one who has changed the winter gloominess into spring brightness?"[39] Bernardi interprets this comment to mean that in Basil's day, Gordius was commemorated in the spring.[40] Another possibility is that the joyousness of the feast lifted their spirits on an otherwise gloomy winter day. An interesting feature of this homily is that it indicates that the martyrdom of Gordius, which took place during the Diocletian persecutions, happened on a pagan feast day, in which the whole town of Caesarea went to the arena to watch chariot races in honor of an unspecified warlike deity.[41] According to Basil, Gordius, "perceiving himself to be fully trained and having anointed himself with oil for the contest by fasts, by sleeplessness, by prayers, by the uninterrupted and unceasing study of the sayings of the Spirit,"[42] took advantage of the fact that most of the populace was gathered together in one place. He ran from the city, past the crowds and into the center of the arena, where, in full view of everyone, he cried out, "'I was found by those who did not seek me. I was manifest to those who did not consult me' (cf. Is. 65.1), revealing through these things," Basil says, "that he was not brought to the dangers with force, but he freely gave himself voluntarily to the contest, having imitated the Master, who in the darkness of the night, not being recognized by the Jews, made himself known."[43] Apparently, this halted the festivities, because Gordius was able to give a lengthy explanation of his faith to those gathered in the arena, and when he was done, he drew the outline of a cross around himself and surrendered to beheading.[44] As Bernardi points out, Basil does not say whether this pagan feast was still being observed in his day,[45] but if it was, it had serious competition from the Christian feast; Basil describes the people of the city pouring out to the "arena of the martyrs" like bees out of a hive.[46]

Gregory of Nyssa composed a homily for the feast of St. Theodore, the soldier. According to Daniélou, the sermon was delivered in 381 either in Amaseia, where Theodore was thought to have been martyred, or in Euchaita, where his relics were believed to have been taken by the Christian princess Eusebia.[47] Gregory indicates that it is winter but does not provide additional clues that might enable us to date the feast more precisely.[48] Gregory of Nazianzus's successor in Constantinople, Nectarius, also preached a sermon on Theodore, attesting the existence of his cult in the imperial city at this time.[49] This Theodore is not mentioned in the SM or the HM, but he is listed in the *Typikon* for June 8.

In addition to these feast days that we can date more or less specifically, the Cappadocians provide evidence of other saints' commemorations that were part of their calendars. Basil attests the existence in Caesarea of a cult of St. Julitta, mother of St. Cyriacus of Iconium. One year her feast day interrupted Basil's two-day exposition of 1 Thessalonians 5.16–18. He had been preaching on this passage the day before[50] but only managed to cover Paul's instruction to "rejoice always."[51] He planned to continue with "pray incessantly" and "be thankful in all things" the next day. However, the next day was the feast of St. Julitta, so Basil opened the sermon with praise of Julitta and then resumed his preaching on the text from 1 Thessalonians.[52]

In trying to date this sermon, Bernardi makes an interesting point about Basil's weaving of the Thessalonians text and the martyr's story. He writes:

> The eulogy of the martyr was intended to provide a particularly striking illustration, since it is a question of a woman, of the attitude that the preacher recommends to his audience to adopt, an attitude of confident joy and of thanksgiving in the midst of the cruelest and most unexpected ordeals. It is significant that, among all the examples mentioned, it is that of a notable woman of Caesarea, a victim of persecution, who is brought most vividly to light. Thus profoundly wedding the themes of the two sermons, the orator clarifies his ulterior motive: his main intention seems to be

to strengthen the part of his audience that is susceptible to being the victim of Valens.[53]

What Bernardi hints at is that the part of the audience Basil seems particularly interested in strengthening is the female component. The words Basil (or the martyrdom account he used as a source) puts into Julitta's mouth are fascinating. Having refused to deny her faith, she was condemned to be burned to death. She ran to the pyre with great joy, but before leaping into the flames, she took the time to speak to the women who were standing nearby, exhorting them not to use the weakness of their nature as an excuse for living ungodly lives. She says:

> We have come into being according to the image of God, as also have they [men]. Womankind has come into being from the creator capable of virtue equally with the male. And *why* are we akin to men forever? For not only was flesh taken for the constitution of woman but also bone from bones. For this reason, the firmness and vigor and endurance are also owed by us equally with men to the Master.[54]

She then jumped into the fire, which killed her but somehow preserved her body; those who were nearby retrieved the body and laid it in "the most beautiful temple precincts in the city," where it, "on the one hand, consecrates the grave and, on the other hand, consecrates the ones who gather in it." Before returning to Thessalonians, Basil says, "Men, do not allow women to appear inferior for piety. Women, do not be deprived of the example, but cling unhesitatingly to piety...because the disadvantage of nature is a hindrance to you for none of the good things."[55]

Basil's homily does not give an indication of date of Julitta's feast day or of the time of year during which it fell, although the HM places it on June 16 and the *Typikon* on July 15.[56] Whatever the date, Bernardi maintains that it was Basil himself who chose it for Julitta. At the beginning of the homily, Basil says, "Περιηγγείλαμεν γὰρ ὑμῖν τὴν ἡμέραν ταύτην, ὡς ὑπόμνημα ἔχουσαν τῆς μεγάλης ἀθλήσεως." Bernardi translates this phrase, "Indeed we have set (περιηγγείλαμεν) you this day as marking the memorial of this great struggle."[57] However, περιαγγέλλω does not mean "to set"; it means "to announce by sending around a message." This *could* mean that Basil had also established the feast day he was announcing, but it does not *necessarily* mean that he did.

Gregory of Nyssa attests the existence of a commemoration of his brother Peter, bishop of Sebaste from 380 or 381 until his death in 391. According to Gregory, this commemoration was already a custom for the faithful there. In a letter written around 393 to Flavian of Antioch, he writes:

> At last after I had concluded the services at Sebastia in commemoration of Peter of most blessed memory, and of the holy martyrs, who had lived in his times, and whom the people were accustomed to commemorate with him, I was returning to my own See, when some one told me that Helladius himself was in the neighbouring mountain district, holding martyrs' memorial services.[58]

The HM lists Peter of Sebaste on March 26, but it does not give the names of any martyrs honored along with him.[59]

In addition to Theodore, Pontus's other major martyr was the innkeeper and gardener Phocas, whose gift of extraordinary hospitality extended even to the soldiers who had been sent to arrest and execute him[60] by beheading in 303. Phocas was born in Sinope, a town on the southern coast of the Black Sea; in his encomium at the martyr's tomb, Asterius tells us, "Indeed, our neighbor Sinope, ancient and well-known city, full of strong and philosophic men, produced the holy man, the great benefit of Christians."[61] Even in Asterius's time Phocas enjoyed more than local notoriety. Asterius says:

> I have gone through these things in order that I might show, he is more conspicuous, as the one who offers to us today the occasion of the assembly for the companions and fellow-combatants. For, on the one hand, not all the others are revealed in the sight of all, nor do they have the bravery that has been proclaimed; on the other hand, there is no one who does not know Phocas, but just as the ray of sun has been spread to all eyes, so the report of this martyr has embraced every ear....[62]

Specifically, Asterius says that Phocas is honored by Scythians and Romans.[63] In fact, he claims that the Romans, who have obtained the head of the martyr, revere him as much as they do Peter and Paul! He says:

> So then also throughout the ruling city, the head of Italy and queen of the world, there is a great bodyguard for him and also value and a conspicuous house, engaged in beauty. But Romans serve Phocas no less than Peter and Paul. And as the word teaches, they earnestly acquired the head of the martyr, having chosen as a token a counterpart of the wanton Herodias.[64]

The *depositio martyrum* of the *Chronograph of 354* does not mention Phocas, so if Asterius is correct about his importance in the Roman cult of martyrs, this must have been a later development. Asterius does not give any indication of the date of this commemoration, but the HM lists Phocas on

February 1. The *Typikon* gives two dates—September 22 and July 22.[65]

Asterius also composed an ecphrasis for St. Euphemia, who was martyred in Chalcedon in 303 or 304. Her martyrium in Chalcedon had already been built by the time the Spanish religious Egeria traveled through the area in the early 380s, because Egeria made a point of stopping there during her journey. She writes:

> I stayed there [Tarsus] three days before setting off to continue my journey, and then, after a day's travelling, arrived at a staging-post called Mansucrene below Mount Taurus, and continued along a road we already knew, since our outward journey had brought us along it. Passing through the same provinces of Cappadocia, Galatia, and Bithynia, I reached Chalcedon, and I stayed there because it contains the renowned martyrium of holy Euphemia, long known to me.[66]

Asterius's work was probably composed before he became a bishop, perhaps even before he was ordained.[67] At the time he wrote the ecphrasis, he was living in Chalcedon, because he says upon growing weary of reading Demosthenes, he walked to the marketplace and reached the church at which a painting of the holy woman stood near her tomb.[68] This is not a sermon for her feast day, but Asterius does indicate that there was an annual festival in her honor in Chalcedon. He writes:

> A certain woman, a consecrated virgin, having dedicated her undefiled self-control to God—we call her Euphemia—very willingly chose the danger in death when a tyrant was carrying off those who were devout; but then the citizens and companions in the religion for which she died, as those who have marveled together at the strong and consecrated virgin, have built themselves the tomb near the sanctuary and have laid up the coffin as a memorial, pay their respects to her and consider the annual feast a communal and public festal gathering. Therefore, the priests of the mysteries of God always honor her memory both by word and by principle, and they thoroughly teach the assembling peoples how diligently she finished the contest of perseverance. And, indeed, the painter, being devout and through skill having himself ably sketched the whole account on his cloth has dedicated a holy sight somewhere around the tomb: and here is the masterpiece.[69]

The HM contains several feast days for Euphemia, especially in Chalcedon. It lists her commemoration in Constantinople on July 3.[70] In the *Typikon* she also has several days—September 16, May 16 and July 11.[71]

Egeria says that she visited "the tombs of the apostles" and "many martyria" while she was in Constantinople,[72] but the surviving works of Gregory of Nazianzus do not provide much information about the sanctoral cycle there during his episcopate.[73] His *Oration 21 On the Great Athanasius, Bishop of Alexandria* was delivered at Constantinople on Athanasius's feast day,[74] probably May 2, 379.[75] His *Oration 24 In Honor of Cyprian*, also preached in Constantinople, refers to the annual feast celebrated there in honor of Cyprian of Carthage,[76] but as Bernardi points out, Gregory seems to confuse Cyprian of Carthage, who was martyred under Valerian and who pre-dated Sabellians and Arians, with some other Cyprian, who wrote refutations of these groups and was martyred in the fourth century. Bernardi suggests Cyprian of Antioch, whose feast day is either October 2 or 4.[77]

Why Feast the Saints?

Asterius's sermon *Against Covetousness* was delivered on the feast day of an unidentified saint. Asterius talks about some of the things that were customarily done at such celebrations and, in so doing, gives us a glimpse of *why*, in his opinion, honoring martyrs was important. He says:

> Christians and sharers of a heavenly calling, you country folk, and all who come from the towns, you who in concord have gathered at the present feast, — for by a general address I embrace you all, — has each one of you thoughtfully considered and realized why we are assembled? And why are martyrs honored by the construction of notable buildings and by these annual assemblies, and what end did our fathers have in view when they ordained the things we see, and left the established custom to their descendants? Is it not evident to one who concentrates his thought on this subject even for a short time, that these things have been given permanent form to rouse us to pious emulation, and that the feasts constitute public schools for our souls, in order that while we honor the martyrs, we may learn to imitate their sturdy piety; that lending the ear to the gathered teachers, we may learn some useful thing which we did not know before,— either the certainty of some doctrine, or the explanation of some difficult Scripture, — or may hear some discourse that will improve our morals?[78]

Not surprisingly, the theme of the saint as model of piety and virtue is a common one in our sermons. In his homily for the feast of St. Theodore, Gregory of Nyssa exhorts his listeners to allow the story of the martyr's sufferings to motivate them to follow his example and to abandon vain pursuits.[79] In his second homily for St. Stephen's day, Gregory points out that merely honoring the saints outwardly is not enough; one must also internalize their virtues by patterning one's own life after those of the martyrs. He asks the faithful, "Do you honor the martyrs' memory and hold them in veneration? Fellowship with their memory implies agreement with their mind."[80]

In addition, Gregory says that hearing about the virtuous deeds is the best way to internalize them. In preaching about the Forty Martyrs of Sebaste, he says, "Beholding their example is fine, but it is better to hear about them because words enable their teaching to enter the soul."[81] For Asterius words are not enough; one has to gaze upon the actual tomb. He opens his sermon on Phocas by saying:

> The commemoration of the saints is good and useful to those who practice the excellent things. For it educates those who desire virtues and godliness not only by word, but it also puts forth the actions of those who have lived uprightly as visible teachers.... And so indeed we pupils of the martyrs, considering as teachers the deeds of strong men in defense of the confession, learn to defend godliness until the last dangers, looking upon their consecrated graves themselves as pillars written with letters and accurately revealing the agony of martyrdom.[82]

Another benefit of remembering and honoring the saints is participation in their healing and protective powers, which are located primarily in their relics but also in their efficacious intercessions. This healing takes place on multiple levels, physical and spiritual. First, contact with and prayer through a martyr's relics effects physical healing, protection and refreshment. Gregory of Nyssa says:

> These spectacles strike the senses and delight the eye by drawing us near to [the martyr's] tomb which we believe to be both a sanctification and blessing. If anyone takes dust from the martyr's resting place, it is a gift and a deserving treasure. Should a person have both the good fortune and permission to touch the relics, this experience is a highly valued prize and seems like a dream both to those who were cured and whose wish was fulfilled. The body appears as if it were alive and healthy: the eyes, mouth, ears as well as the other senses are a cause for pouring out tears of reverence and emotion. In this way one implores the martyr who intercedes on our behalf and is an attendant of God for imparting those favors and blessings which people seek.[83]

Gregory also says that Theodore's tomb was a place of respite from all sorts of afflictions:

> However, [Theodore] left behind a lesson from his agony: he summoned the people, taught the church, put demons to flight, brought angelic peace, implored benefits from God, healed various illnesses in that place, provided a safe haven for those tossed by afflictions, was a rich treasury for the poor, a quiet inn of rest for travellers and a continuous festal celebration. If we keep the yearly festival, an enthusiastic multitude will always be in attendance; the highway leading there bore them along like ants with some going and other [sic] departing.[84]

According to Asterius, Phocas was another such source of sustenance. He claims:

> Ladies and gentlemen, we have this pillar and support of the churches of God from that time until now, and he is the most notable of martyrs, having first place among the best and blessed ones. For 'star differs from star in glory' (I Cor. 15.41), not only according to the common estimate but also according to the sound of the instrument of choice, and indeed above all he is also most famous among the saints everywhere in the world. And he draws and brings all to his resting place, and the highways are full of those from each country who are hastening to the place of prayer. Therefore, indeed, that magnificent temple is relief for the oppressed, provision for the poor, remedy for the afflicted, Egypt for the hungry. And although he has died, Phocas feeds more abundantly than Joseph [did] living; for the latter exchanged grain for silver, but the former gives gifts freely to those who ask.[85]

Sometimes the encounter between supplicant and intercessor is described as a bargaining session. Asterius gives one such account:

> For this reason, having reverently wrapped up the godly bodies, we protect the vessels of choice with our whole life, the instruments of the blessed souls, the houses of the inhabitant philosophers, as highly honored treasures, and we keep watch with them as with our virtues, and the church has been built by the martyrs as a city by armed nobles, and common festal gatherings are assembled, and we enjoy the rejoicing of the feasts. And those who are pressed by human circumstances or misfortunes strive for the reposes of the thrice-blessed ones as for some refuge, considering them ambassadors of the prayers and requests by means of what surpasses freedom to speak. From here needs are done away with and diseases are cured and threats of rulers are calmed; and the holy burial places of the martyrs are calm harbors from all of the commotions and storms of life. So a father or mother, having lifted the sick child and wrapped [it] in her arms runs past remedies and physicians and flees to unskilled help; and, having come to one of the martyrs, brings the request to the Master through him, having inquired of such ones with voices to the mediator: "Since you have suffered on account of Christ, be an ambassador concerning suffering and disease. Even though you have left our life behind, you know the sufferings of humanity; *you* also once appealed to martyrs before becoming a martyr. Then, seeking, you received; now, having, give freely. In your reward, ask gain for us. May we be healed by your wound as the world [was] by that of Christ."[86]

Gregory of Nyssa also attests the existence of the notion that those buried near martyrs' tombs receive some benefit from this close proximity. He describes how the remains of the Forty Martyrs help both the living and the dead, saying:

The bodies have been consumed by flames. We have scattered their ashes and burnt remains, and the entire earth praises these saints. I will share in their merits by placing my parents' bodies beside the remains of these soldiers. In this way they will rise at the resurrection with those who are filled with greater confidence. I know they will prevail because I have witnessed their courage and faith before God.[87]

Second, the healing provided by martyrs went beyond the realm of the physical to include strengthening of souls. In a letter written in 374 to Ascholius, Bishop of Thessalonica, whom Basil addresses as the "trainer" of the martyr Sabas, Basil writes:

But, our souls have returned to that pristine happiness since your letter came from afar blossoming with the beauty of love. Furthermore, a martyr has come to us from the barbarians beyond the Ister. [*sic*] proclaiming through himself the exactness of the faith practiced there. Who could describe the joy of our souls at this? What power of speech could be devised capable of clearly expressing the feelings in the innermost depths of our heart? Truly, when we saw the athlete we congratulated his trainer, who will also receive for himself the crown of justice at the hand of the most just Judge, because he has strengthened many for the contest in defense of religion.[88]

Gregory of Nyssa implores St. Theodore:

We who have been kept safe and unharmed ponder your beneficence and implore protection for the future. Should we experience stress and dishonor, let your people beseech the chorus of your fellow martyrs; the prayers of many just people will exonerate sin.... But by the power of your intercession and those with you, oh marvelous and most bright among the martyrs, the young shoot will return to you, the flourishing citizenship of Christians will endure to the end in the splendid fruitful field of faith in Christ which always bears the fruit of eternal life in Christ Jesus Lord [*sic*].[89]

Gregory also calls the Forty Martyrs "intercessors," who constantly offer prayers on behalf of living Christians and who are powerful allies against opponents. He urges the faithful to rely on these martyrs for assistance in standing firm against temptation, wicked persons and tyrants.[90] Asterius says confidently, "For the very good hope of the good and noetic ones is a teacher of courage and perseverance, which [hope] being involved in the accounts as a trustworthy security and safe deposit exhorts everyone to look at danger undauntedly and to endure the trial nobly; and this consequently happens."[91] Later in the same sermon, he says, "For since our prayer is not sufficient to entreat God in time of distress or misfortune—for our entreaty is not an appeal but a remembrance of sins—for this reason we flee for refuge to the fellow slaves who are loved by God, in order that they in their own perfections might heal our faults."[92]

Third, the healing and protection afforded by the martyrs was believed to extend to communities and nations. When the Scythians were threatening to attack, Gregory of Nyssa requested aid from St. Theodore, appropriately enough, praying on behalf of those gathered for the saint's festival:

> We beseech you, whether you dwell in the air above or in some celestial circle or angelic chorus, that you assist the Lord or worship him as a faithful servant with the powers and virtues. Come from that place to those who beseech you, invisible friend! You have learned of his death, a means by which you might give double thanks to God who conferred this favor through one passion and one pious confession that you may rejoice in the blood he shed and in the grievous fire he endured. As a result you will have as worthy ministers those who witnessed the spectacle. We lack many benefactors. Intercede on behalf of the people that they may share one kingdom because the martyr's country is one of affliction whose citizens and brethren and kinsmen have died and have been honored. We fear afflictions and expect danger because we are close to the ungodly Sythians [sic] who grieve us with war. As a soldier, fight for us; as a martyr, grant courage to your fellow servants. Since you have prevailed over this life yet are familiar with humanity's sufferings and needs grant peace that the festivals may continue, that the furious, insolent, mad barbarians might not triumph over the temples or altars and that they might not tread the holy place.[93]

The martyrs apparently provided protection not only against barbarian invasion but also against persecution. In a letter written in 373 to an unspecified "trainer," Basil writes:

> Now, whatever good deeds you do personally you store up as a treasure for yourself; whatever relief you offer to those who suffer persecution for the name of the Lord, this you prepare for yourself on the day of recompense. And you will do well if you send the relics of the martyrs to your native country, since, as you wrote to us, the persecution there is even now making martyrs to the Lord.[94]

Interestingly, however, the cult of martyrs also provided a healing of ethnic and geographical divisions, drawing together otherwise disparate groups. After describing how Phocas, who had been a gardener, became the patron saint of sailors, Asterius says that kings and barbarians are also amazed by the martyr's protective powers. Then he says:

> ...and all the wildest Scythians, indeed all who possess the land opposite the sea of Euxine [Black Sea], dwelling near the Palus Maeotis [Sea of Azof] and the river

Tanaidos, and all who inhabit the Bosphorus and are extended as far as the river Phasis, all these attend to the gardener; but having separated from us in all the customs and ways of life, in this only do they become like-minded, taming their wildness of conduct by the truth.[95]

This idea that martyrs' relics had the power to unite individuals or groups was more than just a homiletic device. In the final section of this chapter, we will explore how veneration of relics and celebration of saints' days were used to form alliances, particularly alliances against those whose teachings they considered heretical.

Martyrs as Allies

The martyrs were used both physically and rhetorically to solidify friendships, to forge alliances against heretics and other opponents and to refute those opponents. The Cappadocians participated enthusiastically in these activities. For example, in 375 Basil sent Ambrose of Milan the remains of one of Ambrose's predecessors, Dionysius, who became bishop of Milan in 346. Although Dionysius was not technically a martyr, he was exiled by Emperor Constantius to Cappadocia, where he died in 374, a casualty in the war being waged between Catholics and Arians. Ambrose wrote to Basil requesting that Dionysius's body be returned to Milan, a request with which Basil complied, although the bodyguards of the tomb and the priests and faithful who frequented it were not as easy to convince. The letter Basil wrote to accompany these relics shows that he considered this a cementing of an already-cordial relationship between like-minded persons. He writes:

Always magnificent and abundant are the gifts of our Lord, and neither can their magnitude be measured nor their quantity numbered. But, one of the greatest gifts to those keenly aware of receiving His favors is this present one – that He has granted us, though far separated by the position of our countries, to be united with each other through the declarations in our letters.[96]

That Ambrose revered Dionysius was evidence that he was the right kind of Christian. Basil continues:

Your loving esteem and zeal for the most blessed Bishop Dionysius give evidence of your perfect love for the Lord, your respect for your predecessors, and your earnestness concerning the faith. For, our disposition toward the well-disposed of our fellow servants is referable to the Lord, whom they have served, and he who honors those who have gone through struggles for the faith is clearly possessed of an equal zeal for the faith, so that one act in itself bears testimony of much virtue.[97]

Basil also took great care to assure Ambrose of the authenticity of the relics he was sending. He writes:

Receive these relics with as much joy as was the grief of the guards who sent them forward. Let no one hesitate, let no one doubt: this is that unconquerable athlete. The Lord knows these bones which struggled to the end with the blessed soul. He will crown these bones with this soul on the just day of His retribution.... There was one coffin which had received that honored body; no one else was laid near him; his burial was a notable one; his honor that of a martyr. Christians who had entertained him as a guest buried him with their own hands then, and now took him up. They cried as if bereaved of a father and a leader; but they sent him on, preferring your joy to their own consolation. Those, therefore, who handed him over are pious; those who received him are scrupulously careful. Nowhere is there falsehood, nowhere deceit—we ourselves bear witness; let the truth be free from misrepresentation in your presence.[98]

Clearly, there was traffic in fake relics, and Basil was concerned to uphold his reputation. His rhetoric also subtly puts Ambrose in his debt—and in the debt of the Cappadocians who were deprived of Dionysius's holy bones and, therefore, healing and protective services.

A few years earlier, Basil planned to solidify his relationship with Bishop Arcadius in a similar way. In a letter composed around 370, Basil writes:

We were delighted beyond measure that, upon yourself assuming a charge becoming to a Christian, you had erected a home for the glory of the name of Christ, truly loving, as it is written, 'the beauty of the house of the Lord.' [cf ps. 26.8] Doing so, you have provided for yourself the heavenly mansion which is prepared in the place of rest for those who love the name of the Lord. If we are able to find relics of martyrs anywhere, we beg that we also may contribute to your undertaking. For, if 'the just shall be in everlasting remembrance,' [Ps. 112.6] surely we shall be sharers of the good remembrance which will be given to you by the saint.[99]

Notice that Basil's *expressed* reason for wanting to locate some relics to contribute to Arcadius's church was that he might participate in the saint's distribution of blessings.

Basil gave some of the relics of the Forty Martyrs of Sebaste to a group of nuns in Caesarea, who, in turn, gave them to Gaudentius of Brescia as an expression of solidarity. Peter Brown writes:

Gaudentius of Brescia is one example of the new type of traveler. A wealthy man of ascetic leanings and strong antipathy to the Arian views then dominant in northern Italy, Gaudentius had decided to travel to the Holy Land. In Cappadocia he had received from the nuns of Caesarea relics of the forty martyrs of Sebaste, which they had received from none other than Saint Basil [Gaudentius Sermon 17, PL 20.965A]. The community had 'deigned to bestow' these on him as 'faithful companions' of his journey:[964A] and solidarity [965A]. Gaudentius echoed the gesture on his return. He called the church in which he placed these and other relics in Brescia "The Gathering of the Saints," *concilium sanctorum* [971A]. Preaching in around 387 at a time when only a few of his colleagues had been able to travel to Brescia for fear of an impending barbarian invasion [960A], his "Church of the Gathering of the Saints" stood out, for Gaudentius, as a monument of happier days of ideal solidarity in a less dislocated world."[100]

Basil was also the *recipient* of such gifts. In 374 he wrote a letter that is addressed to "a trainer" but probably intended for Basil's kinsman Soranus, Duke of Scythia. He writes:

But, further, what are your present deeds? With the body of a martyr who lately finished his struggle in the barbarous neighboring land, you have honored the country which bore you, like a grateful farmer sending back the first fruits to those who supplied the seeds. The gifts are truly becoming to an athlete of Christ—a martyr of the truth, recently crowned with the crown of righteousness—and we not only received it rejoicing, but also glorified God who has already caused the Gospel of His Christ to be observed among all the nations.[101]

Although neither side possessed the actual relics of Stephen, both sides in the debate over the divinity of the Holy Spirit claimed him as an ally, according to Gregory of Nyssa. On the feast of Stephen, he exhorted his flock to reject the Pneumatomachian interpretation of Acts 7.55, which claimed the Holy Spirit's apparent absence from Stephen's vision of the Godhead as scriptural warrant for denying the divinity of the Holy Spirit. Gregory, of course, saw this as a misinterpretation and as proof that his opponents lacked the indwelling of the Spirit.[102]

Asterius of Amaseia uses his encomium on all the martyrs as an opportunity to refute both pagans and Eunomians, who have accused the martyr-loving Christians of worshiping dead human bodies. Asterius responds:

We do not worship martyrs, but we honor [them] as genuine worshipers of God; we do not worship humans, but we admire those who have worshiped God rightly in time of trials. We bury [them] in beauty-loving graves, and we erect magnificent houses with preparations of their resting place, in order that we might desire the

> honors of those who have died well; we do not show unpaid zeal to them, but we
> enjoy their protection that is near God.[103]

He asks the pagans how they, who do not honor dead humans but worship them as gods, have the nerve to make such an accusation, when honoring martyrs simply represents an eagerness to please God and a fleeing to
patrons for refuge.[104] He asks, "Did you not by your own folly deify Demeter
and Kore, and build for yourself two temples made to women, and you honor
them with sacrifices and worship them with manifold services? Is not the
main point of your cult the mysteries in Eleusis, and the Attic populace and
all of Greece stream together, in order that you might perform emptiness for
yourself?"[105] He describes the cults of Dionysius, Silenus, Heracles and
Asclepius and continues:

> For everywhere in the inhabited earth there are temples that have been raised up, I
> mean the festival of Asclepius and the festival of Heracles and the festival of
> Dionysius, exalted proofs of your emptiness have stood; and so I, on the one hand,
> will depart guiltless from the accusation, for I do not worship martyrs nor think
> [them to be] gods; but you, on the other hand, being subject to the accusations and
> accusing these things of others have renounced, just like those who are the first ac-
> cusers of the innocent on account of evil complicity. For you have been exposed as
> worshiping humans as gods.[106]

Asterius also rebukes the followers of Eunomius, who taught that the
persons of the Godhead were of unlike substance. For Eunomius, God is
ἀγεννησία (ungenerate) but completely comprehensible and is a single substance that abhors distinctions of both properties and attributes. The Son is
not generated within the Divine Nature but produced by the Father. The Holy
Spirit is the first creation of the Son and the means by which the Son sancti-
fies souls. Eunomius also "taught that piety does not consist in the invocation
of holy names or in the use of rites and symbols, but in exactitude of doctrine, teaching which necessarily led to the disregard of the Sacraments and
of ascetical practices." [107] Apparently, this rejection of the tangible also extended to the practice of honoring martyrs. Asterius says to those who follow
Eunomius's teachings:

> But Jews of the new rebellion, what wonder is it if you dishonor martyrs, when you
> reject Christ and separate [him] from his likeness to the Father in your own words,
> and avoid as profane the places in which holy bodies have taken their rest? But you
> who did not come into knowledge of the one who came to be, be afraid, so-called
> Christians, hating martyrs with the Greeks. Do you not know, as Christ the chief

martyr who suffered first and then sent forth the zeal to the slaves? Then, after him, Stephen, the champion named after the godly honor; then all the disciples and apostles. And observe how many you dishonor through a single arrogance: John the Baptist, James called the brother of the Lord, Peter, Paul, Thomas—I name these as leaders of the martyrs—, then the boundless multitude of those who died in behalf of the life.[108]

Asterius calls them "the evil army of heretics that now wickedly wearies our life and does not respect the martyrs with the magnificence of the wonders" and continues, interceding with the saints on behalf of these opponents:

...but they name places where people assemble and tombs and their deaths, and they loathe the entrances themselves as being rubbed against by defilements, and not remembering that God-inspired word from every song-filled mouth, that 'Precious before the Lord [is] the death of his holy ones.' Let us pray to God, therefore, and let us summon martyrs to entreat the communal Master, in order that a spirit of contrition might be given to those who are being worked by the wandering heretic....[109]

Like Gregory of Nyssa, Asterius also uses the feast of Stephen to refute opponents, but in this case the heretics in question are Sabellians as well as Pneumatomachians. Sabellians were modalistic monarchians who believed that the Godhead was a monad expressed in three operations; the Father was the essence, who self-expressed in the modes of Son and Spirit like the sun self-expresses in the modes of heat and light.[110] Asterius uses Stephen's vision to refute this "confusion of the substances":

But it is not proper to leave behind the vision of Stephen unexamined, for the God of all things, always providing for the next of the failures that are to come in the life of humans, protectively prepares the cure beforehand, which indeed he has also done here. For if the vision of God was accomplished to the benefit of the champion only, it was enough for the voice to come out of the heavens, just as first at the time of the baptism or in later years at the time of the Transfiguration or even as in the time of this Paul, when he was traveling to Damascus. But now on account of the Sabellian evil from Libya that is about to attack the churches of God and to bring the heretical confusion of the substances into the life, for this reason God, as it were cutting the future away first and later securing the souls, shows himself to Stephen in his own and perfect glory, but he also shows the Son in perfected person, and he causes him to stand at his own right hand in order that by means of elucidation he might articulate the substance of the persons.[111]

Asterius does not specifically address the Pneumatomachian interpretation of the account of Stephen's martyrdom, as Gregory of Nyssa did, but he does address the apparent absence of the Holy Spirit in Stephen's vision. If

God was so concerned to convey correct christology in this vision, why did God not also communicate correct pneumatology? He tells those who might be wondering about this to consider the larger context of the story. He says:

> And perhaps someone will say: he has thus philosophized the things about the Father and the Son, but where is the holy Spirit? For if the Father made an appearance with the Son from heaven for the sake of certainty with respect to faith, it was necessary that the holy Spirit also be present in order that some effective mystagogy be accomplished for humans through the vision. So it is necessary to say to the one who replies to us with this understanding, "Oh, most clever one, it is necessary that the examiner of the readings together have both the correct understanding and vigorous memory, in order that he might thus be able to grasp all of the written things together. For if you also seek the presence of the Spirit, be above the stones and bloodthirstiness for a moment, and you will find the Spirit before the vision, speaking to and being present with Stephen and getting the athlete ready."[112]

A dynamic of relationship building with visible and invisible allies is evident in the practices and homilies of our preachers. Their non-homiletical works are also to a large degree about refuting the teachings of their opponents; however, the pulpit and the martyrium were probably the sites at which they had the most contact with the faithful, with whom they were also concerned to build relationships and forge alliances. It is interesting that the feast of Stephen was a particularly useful site for polemical activity. Gregory of Nyssa says that the scriptural account of Stephen's martyrdom, in which Stephen's vision was of the Father and the Son only, was one of the points used by the Pneumatomachians in their case against the divinity of the Holy Spirit. This would have made this feast the perfect opportunity to refute opposing pneumatology and to teach "right belief."

Notes

1. Asterius of Amaseia, *Encomium in sanctos martyres* 1.1–2.
2. Gregory of Nyssa, *Life of Gregory the Wonderworker* 14.95, in *St. Gregory Thaumaturgus: Life and Works*, trans. Michael Slusser, The Fathers of the Church, ed. Thomas P. Halton *et al.* (Washington, D.C.: The Catholic University of America Press, 1998), 83.
3. Sozomen, *The Ecclesiastical History* 5.11.
4. Basil of Caesarea, Letter C, *NPNF*, Series 2, vol. 8, 184.
5. Ibid., Letter CXLII, *NPNF*, 205.
6. Ibid., Letter CLXXVI, *NPNF*, 220.
7. Ibid., Letter CCLII, *NPNF*, 292.

8. Delehaye claims that the HM places this commemoration on September 10 (Delehaye, *Origines*, 176), but this is incorrect. The saints honored in Caesarea on that day, according to the HM are the martyrs Euplia (or Euphepia, in one of the recensions), Alexander, Cupsicus, Hysicus, Alapon, Silvanus *cum aliis* and the bishop Salvius (HM, 119). The HM's entry for September 8 says, "*IN EADEM DIE collectio ceserea cappadocie. et totius terreturii*" ("ON THE SAME DAY a gathering in Caesarea of Cappadocia and of the entire surrounding area)" (HM, 118). Delehaye maintains that the manuscripts must be defective at this point and that its original form must have been "*Caesarea Cappadociae Eupsichii, Dama et multorum martyrum collectio totius territorii.*" This would resolve the problem of the lack of saints given to be commemorated by this *collectio*, but Delehaye does not say *why* the reconstruction of the text should include Eupsychius and his companions. In any case, that date still does not agree with the testimony of Basil.

9. SM, LIII.

10. *Typikon* I,19.

11. Basil of Caesarea, *Homilia in Mamantem Martyrem* 4.

12. Talley, *Origins*, 96. Bernardi (85) and Fedwick (10, n. 47) date this sermon to September 2, perhaps because of this passage or perhaps because that is the date assigned to Mamas in the *Typikon* (I, 11). However, as Talley points out, the beginning of the civil year did not shift to September 1 until the fifth century, so it is difficult to determine the precise date with absolute certainty.

13. Bernardi, 251.

14. Gregory of Nazianzus, *In novam Dominicam* 12.

15. Bernardi, 85, n. 166.

16. Gregory of Nazianzus, Letter 122, *NPNF*, Series 2, vol. 7, 472.

17. SM, LXI; *Typikon* I, 51.

18. Gregory of Nazianzus, *The Panegyric on S. Basil* 58.

19. Delehaye, 176: *L'église de Tyane en Cappadoce fut illustrée par le martyre de S. Oreste. La Passion* (BHG², 1383; Act. SS., Nov. t. IV, p. 391–99) *raconte que son corps, jeté dans les flots, fut recueilli par les fidèles et enseveli sur la montagne voisine de la ville, où il continua à guérir les malades.*

20. HM, 86.

21. Gregory of Nyssa, *On Saint Stephen* I, *GNH; GNO* 10.1.2, 75.6–7.

22. Asterius of Amaseia, *Laudatio S. protomartyris Stephani* 1.2.

23. A.G. Martimort, I.H. Dalmais, P. Jounel, eds., *The Church at Prayer*, Vol. IV: *The Liturgy and Time*, trans. Matthew J. O'Connell (Collegeville, MN: The Liturgical Press, 1986), 114–115. I am grateful to the Reverend Dr. John Baldovin for bringing this point to my attention.

24. Gregory of Nyssa, *On Saint Stephen* II, *GNH; GNO* 10.1.2, 98.19–24.

25. Ibid., *GNO* 10.1.2, 104.8–10.

26. Gregory of Nyssa, *A Eulogy for Basil the Great*, *GNH; GNO* 10.1.2, 109.15–110.5.

27. SM, LII.

28. HM, 1.

29. HM, 1, 3. Interestingly, fifth-century Jerusalem had a slightly different arrangement; the Armenian lectionaries list Stephen on December 27, Peter and Paul on December 28, James and John on December 29 (Baldovin, 284).

30. HM, 2.
31. Ibid.
32. Ibid., 3
33. *Typikon* I, 163, 167.
34. Gregory of Nyssa, *Concerning the Forty Martyrs* II, *GNO* 10.1.2, 166.16–17.
35. Gregory of Nyssa, *In XL Martyres Ib, GNO*, 152.11–13.
36. Gregory of Nyssa, *In XL Martyres II, GNO*, 168.5–10.
37. HM, 30; *Typikon* I, 245.
38. *Typikon* I, 173.
39. Basil, *In Gordium martyrem* 1.
40. Bernardi, 80.
41. Basil, *In Gordium martyrem* 3.
42. Ibid.
43. Ibid.
44. Ibid. 8.
45. Bernardi, 80.
46. Basil of Caesarea, *In Gordium martyrem* 1.
47. Daniélou, "Chronologie," 355, 372.
48. Gregory of Nyssa, *De Sancto Theodoro; GNO* 10.1.2., 61.8–11.
49. *Patrologia Graeca* 39. 1821–1840.
50. Basil of Caesarea, *De gratiarum actione.*
51. Bernardi, 78.
52. Basil of Caesarea, *In martyrem Julittam* 3.
53. Bernardi, 79: *L'éloge de la martyre était destiné à fournir une illustration particulièrement frappante, puisqu'il a'agit d'une femme, de l'attitude que le prédicateur recommande à son public d'adopter, attitude de joie confiante et de remerciement au milieu des épreuves les plus cruelles et les plus inattendues. Il es significatif que, parmi tous les exemples évoqués, ce soit celui d'une notable de Césarée, victime de la persécution, qui soit mis le plus vivement en lumière. Mariant ainsi profondément les thèmes de ses deux sermons, l'orateur éclaire son arrière-pensée: son intention maîtresse semble être d'affermir la partie de son public qui est susceptible d'être la victime de Valens.*
54. Basil of Caesarea, *In martyrem Julittam* 2.
55. Ibid.
56. HM, 79; *Typikon* I, 339.
57. Bernardi, 78. «*Nous vous avons en effet fixé* (περιηγγείλαμεν) *ce jour comme marquant le souvenir de cette grande lutte*» (HD V, 237 A).
58. Gregory of Nyssa, Letter 18, *NPNF*, Series 2, vol. 5, 545.
59. HM, 36.
60. Asterius of Amaseia, *In S. Martyrem Phocam* 7–8.
61. Ibid.5.
62. Ibid. 4.
63. Ibid.12.
64. Ibid. 10.
65. HM, 16; *Typikon* I, 43, 349.
66. Egeria 23.7, *Egeria's Travels*, ed. and trans., John Wilkinson (London: SPCK,

1971), 122.

67. Datema, *Asterius*, xxi.
68. Asterius of Amaseia, *Enarratio in martyrium praeclarissimae martyris Euphemiae* 1–2.
69. Ibid. 2.
70. HM, 86.
71. *Typikon* I, 37, 295, 337.
72. Egeria 23.9, Wilkinson, 122.
73. John Baldovin points out that in fourth-century Constantinople, there would have been very few martyria, given the fact that the imperial city had very few "authentic martyrs of its own" (Baldovin, 209).
74. Gregory of Nazianzus, *Or.* 21.5.
75. Bernardi, 155.
76. Gregory of Nazianzus, *Or.* 24.1.
77. Bernardi, 161.
78. Asterius of Amaseia, *Against Covetousness* 1, *Ancient Sermons*, 75–76.
79. Gregory of Nyssa, *De Sancto Theodoro*; *GNO* 10.1.2, 64.19–22.
80. Gregory of Nyssa, *On Saint Stephen* II, *GNH*; *GNO* 10.1.2, 105.17–23.
81. Gregory of Nyssa, *Concerning the Forty Martyrs* II, *GNH*; *GNO* 10.1.2, 159.15–19.
82. Asterius of Amaseia, *In S. Martyrem Phocam* 1.
83. Gregory of Nyssa, *In Praise of Blessed Theodore, the Great Martyr*, GNH; *GNO* 10.1.2, 63.15–64.2
84. Ibid., *GNH*; *GNO* 10.1.2, 69.21–70.5.
85. Asterius of Amaseia, *In S. Martyrem Phocam* 9.1–3.
86. Ibid., *Encomium in sanctos martyres* 4.1–3.
87. Gregory of Nyssa, *Concerning the Forty Martyrs* II, *GNH*; *GNO* 10.1.2,166.7–13.
88. Basil of Caesarea, Letter 164, *FOTC* I, 324.
89. Gregory of Nyssa, *In Praise of Blessed Theodore, the Great Martyr*, GNH; *GNO* 10.1.2, 70.29–71.16.
90. *In XL Martyres* II; *GNO* 10.1.2, 169.8–22.
91. Asterius of Amaseia, *Encomium in sanctos martyres* 3.1.
92. Ibid. 8.2.
93. Gregory of Nyssa, *In Praise of Blessed Theodore, the Great Martyr*, GNH; *GNO* 10.1.2, 70.6–28.
94. Basil of Caesarea, Letter 155, *FOTC* I, 308.
95. Asterius of Amaseia, *In S. Martyrem Phocam* 12.2.
96. Basil of Caesarea, Letter 197, *FOTC* II, 42.
97. Ibid., 43.
98. Ibid., 44–45.
99. Ibid., Letter 49, *FOTC* I, 130–131.
100. Brown, 95.
101. Basil of Caesarea, Letter 165, *FOTC* I, 327.
102. Gregory of Nyssa, *In Sanctum Stephanum* 1; *GNO* 10.1.2, 89.2–19.
103. Asterius of Amaseia, *Encomium in sanctos martyres* 8.1.
104. Ibid.
105. Ibid. 9.1.

106. Ibid. 9.3.
107. *Oxford Dictionary of the Christian Church*, 2d ed., s.v. "Eunomius."
108. Asterius of Amaseia, *Encomium in sanctos martyres* 10.1–2.
109. Ibid. 18.5–6.
110. J.N.D. Kelly, *Early Christian Doctrines*, rev. ed. (San Francisco: Harper, 1978), 122.
111. Asterius of Amaseia, *Laudatio S. protomartyris Stephani* 12.1–2.
112. Ibid. 13.1–2.

Chapter 5

Conclusions

The main purpose of this project has been to gather the liturgical year data from a group of important Christian preachers who worked in Cappadocia and environs during the fourth and early fifth centuries and to see whether this body of sources sustains current generally-accepted scholarly opinion about liturgical year developments in the East at that time. The answer is, of course, yes and no.

In Chapter 2 we sketched out as clear a picture as possible of paschal festal practice in fourth-century Cappadocia and Pontus. We found that some churches in these provinces probably were among the communities known as Quartodeciman. In fact, although these provinces were among those of the Orient who, according to Constantine's letter, complied with the directives of Nicea in this matter, in Cappadocia there was still some Quartodeciman resistance to Sunday observance of Easter as late as the last quarter of the fourth century. Surprisingly, Nyssa may have been one of these pockets of resistance. In addition, we found enough evidence to suggest that although the disintegration of an earlier unitive Pascha was underway, there was still some resistance, at least rhetorically, to this breakdown in some areas. The disintegration of an earlier unitive season of Pentecost (if, in fact, such a thing ever existed) was more complete by this period in most of the areas covered by this study. There is evidence of a Feast of the Ascension observed forty days after Pascha, although there is no indication that at some earlier time Christ's ascension was part of the fiftieth-day observances, and Pentecost is overwhelmingly described as a single day, devoted to the commemoration of the descent of the Holy Spirit. Lent was a forty-day period rhetorically, but in actuality it consisted of seven weeks of five fasting days per week. There is no indication in our sources of whether or not Holy Week was considered one of these weeks, nor is there mention of a separation of those two fasts by two days of feasting.

Therefore, a general sketch of the paschal cycle of these areas by the beginning of the fifth century includes a seven-week Lent (with no indication of a separation between Lenten and Paschal fasts), a Triemeron (sometimes referred to as a unity, sometimes as two or three separate days), the Pascha (celebrated during a night vigil and during the following day), an Octave, a Feast of the Ascension on the fortieth day after the Pascha (at least in Nyssa), and a Feast of Pentecost (primarily a single day commemorating the descent of the Holy Spirit).

In Chapter 3 we examined the widely-held opinion that Gregory of Nazianzus instituted December 25 as the feast of the Nativity at Constantinople—and the commonly-made inference that, therefore, Constantinople was the first community to celebrate such a feast in this area. Although it cannot be proven conclusively, there is enough evidence at least to suggest that Basil and Caesarea might have been the innovators. In any case, by the middle of the 380s, the December 25 feast had been adopted in Constantinople, Nyssa and Amaseia, and in Iconium by the 390s. We cannot determine how its adoption affected the festal content of the earlier January 6 feast, because we do not possess pre-Christmas evidence that is undeniably about January 6. However, by the time both feasts are irrefutably in the calendars of these areas, December 25 marks the birth of Christ and January 6 commemorates his baptism. Herod's slaughter of the Bethlehemite boys was sometimes included in the events discussed around Christ's nativity, but it was just as often left out; there is no evidence that the Holy Innocents had a commemoration of their own at this time in Cappadocia or Pontus, as they did in Jerusalem.

In summary, a synthesized picture of the Nativity/Incarnation cycle in these areas by the 390s includes a Feast of the Nativity (referred to as either τὰ Θεοφάνια or τὰ Γενέθλια on December 25, and a Feast of Lights (called either τὰ Φῶτα or, more often, ἡ Ἐπιφάνια) on January 6. Feasts of Stephen, John and James, and Paul occurred in the days following τὰ Γενέθλια; although they technically belong in our artificial Sanctoral cycle, in our sermons they are often linked rhetorically to the Nativity feast. Although the Nativity sermons demonstrate a growing interest in the life and virginity of Mary, there is no evidence of a Presentation/Purification feast (or any other Marian feasts) in this area at this time.

In Chapter 4 we assembled the surviving data about feasts of martyrs and saints celebrated in these areas at this time. In his book about the origins and development of the cult of the martyrs, Delehaye notes, "At first, each Church honored its own martyrs, to the exclusion of the others; this was, for each community, a series of family anniversaries. Already in the first half of the fourth century we note borrowings from other Churches."[1] Our sources from Cappadocia and Pontus demonstrate both strata. The precedence of local saints is attested; Basil, especially, concentrates on Caesarean notables such as Eupsychius and Julitta. However, saints and martyrs of universal importance, such as Stephen, John, and James, were also commemorated, and those martyred in nearby cities had also been adopted. For example, Gregory of Nyssa traveled to Armenia Minor to preach on the Forty Martyrs of Sebaste on their home turf, but Basil also composed a sermon honoring these martyrs that was delivered in Caesarea.[2] In addition, at least according to Asterius, Pontus was also *exporting* commemorations; Phocas had become the patron saint of many groups and was honored in many different areas of the world.

We cannot reconstruct a general Sanctoral cycle for the area, because the cults of the martyrs were still highly localized at this time. For Caesarea, we have established feasts for Eupsychius on September 7, Mamas on either September 1 or 23, Gordius in the winter, the Forty Martyrs of Sebaste in early spring, Julitta on an unspecified day. According to Gregory of Nazianzus, Basil also traveled to the outskirts of Tyana in order to celebrate the feast of Orestes. Gregory of Nyssa indicates that his community commemorated the protomartyr Stephen on the day after Christmas and the apostles James, John, Peter and Paul in the days immediately following that. He traveled to Armenia Minor to celebrate the feast of the Forty Martyrs of Sebaste around the beginning of Lent and to attend the commemoration of his brother Peter on an unspecified day. He went to either Amaseia or Euchaita to commemorate Theodore the General. Gregory promoted days honoring his brothers Basil and Peter and says that such days were already a part of the annual cycles of feasts in Caesarea and Sebaste, respectively. Asterius tells us that Stephen was also commemorated on the day after Christmas in Amaseia, and attests the existence of feast days for Phocas and All the Martyrs. Asterius knew of a feast day for Euphemia from his days in Chalcedon but does not say whether he imported her commemoration to Amaseia. Gregory of Nazianzus attests the existence of a feast honoring Athanasius in Constantinople, but his homily in praise of Cyprian is confusing as to which Cyprian was intended. Theodore the General was also honored in Constantinople, as Gregory's successor, Nectarius, indicates.

Feasting Correctly, Relating Suitably, Believing Rightly

In addition to the main goal of gathering the data and reconstructing the annual cycles of the areas under investigation, we have also attempted to view the gathered data in light of the ecclesio-political and cultural context in which they were produced. In each chapter we have focused this lens on a particular group of feasts. This final section is an attempt at a synthesis of our findings.

In a sermon for the feast of Epiphany, newly adopted in the West in his time, Augustine of Hippo complains:

> It's what you would expect, that the Donatist heretics have never been willing to celebrate this day with us; because they have no love for unity, and are not in communion with the Eastern Church, where that star appeared. Let us, though, celebrate in the unity of the nations the manifestation of our Lord and Savior Jesus Christ, by which he picked the firstfruits of the nations.[3]

The Cappadocian sources we have examined do not contain such criticisms of the festal decisions and practices of other Christian groups. If our preachers contrast right Christian feasting with feasting they consider inappropriate, their target of choice is the pagans. We have noted this especially in the critiques of pagan solstice and new year revels in the sermon of Gregory of Nazianzus for the Feast of Lights, in Gregory of Nyssa's letter to Libanius and in the sermon of Asterius of Amaseia against the excesses of the pagan celebration of the kalends of January. In addition to warning about the immorality inherent in such feasts, Asterius gives two other reasons for rejecting this form of celebration. He says:

> Of a public feast, this, then, should be the rule and law: first, that the festival have a distinct object; and then that the mirth be common to all; not that a part enjoy themselves and the rest be left in dejection and pain. For this latter condition is characteristic of war rather than of a feast, since it is inevitable that the victors parade in their victory, while the conquered bewail their misfortune. Now in these days, first, it is not clear for what object this festival is celebrated. For the many legends current concerning it are mutually subversive and disclose nothing certain. Then I see only a few making merry, while the mass of the people are melancholy, even though they try to conceal their dejection by a cheerful demeanor; while all is noise and tumult, the multitude heedlessly jostling one another.[4]

Asterius's second concern is about more than just feasting correctly; it is about relating to one another correctly. He believes that the general gift giving that happens at the new year builds wrong relationships instead of true friendships. He continues:

> It is a recollection of, and a rejoicing over, the new year. What kind of rejoicing, sir? First, then, I observe the manner of meeting, of what a sort it is, and how suspicious and unfriendly! With a voice feeble and faint the salutation drops from the lips. Then follows the kiss, as a prelude to the New Year's present. The mouth indeed is kissed, but it is the coin that is loved, — the form of a sale and the deed of covetousness! But where there is pure and frank friendship, kindnesses are freely bestowed with no expectation of gain. So, while on this New Year's festival many things are carried about everywhere, and money is given, there is no pretext of legitimate barter, nor does any one claim it.... What then are we to call the festival, or the money spent in it? I cannot make out. But tell me, you who have been wearing yourselves out in preparing for it. Give an account of it, as we do of the festivals which are genuine and according to the will of God.[5]

Notice, however, that Asterius does not outlaw gift giving entirely. In fact, we have seen several examples of ambiguity about such activity. Our preachers criticize the prevailing gift economy, especially as it was manifest during the celebration of the kalends of January, yet they participated in a "Christianized" gift economy, in which gifts of letters, treatises and martyrs' bones forged alliances, solidified friendships and created relationships of obligation in an insecure world where the change of emperor could, and often did, mean loss of position and, sometimes, loss of life. Asterius recommended giving gifts of kindness, which are proof of "true friendship," instead of gifts of money, which establish unjust relationships. Gregory of Nyssa gave gifts of his own letters and other writings and considered those he received from others to be more valuable than the gifts of gold given by the pagans. Basil's gift of choice was the relics of martyrs.

Although the Cappadocians did not criticize the festal practices of their Christian opponents, they *did* use some of the annual feasts—as they used many occasions—as opportunities to criticize their opponents' doctrinal teachings, as well as to promote their own teachings, to define "us" and "them" and to establish the beliefs necessary in order for a person to be considered "ours." It has been suggested that the new features of the Cappadocian calendar in this period, namely, Christmas and Ascension, were consciously adopted or created to combat heresy. The data do not sustain this suggestion, although they also do not rule it out. What the data *do* show is that certain times of the year lent themselves to promoting certain doctrines about the persons of the Trinity. Interestingly, the primary loci of the polemic are Christmas, Pentecost and the feast of Stephen. We have seen that whether or not the Feast of the Ascension was established in Cappadocia on the fortieth day after Easter as a conscious attempt to promote the divinity of the Holy Spirit by giving its own feast on the fiftieth day, Pentecost *had* become such a feast, and some of our preachers *did* use its focus on the Holy Spirit to refute Pneumatomachian pneumotology and to teach "right belief." We have also seen that whether or not the Nativity feast of December 25 was adopted as a conscious attempt to promote Nicene christology, our preachers *did* use its focus on the incarnation to refute Arian denial of the Son's consubstantiality with the Father and to teach "right belief." We have also seen that the feast of Stephen, whose scriptural account apparently slights the Holy Spirit, *was* used to refute Pneumatomachian pneumatology and Sabellian anthropology.

In addition to spelling out the differences between right and wrong belief, this is relationship-building rhetoric. It is a fostering of internal cohesion within Christian communities living alongside other Christian communities with different—and threatening—beliefs, but as we have seen, there is more to it than correctly understanding the relationship among the persons of the Trinity or being in right relationship to an orthodox community. In the time period under investigation, the promulgations of Nicea had still not been universally accepted, and the Council of Constantinople happened right around the time that most of our preachers flourished. The emperors were predominantly Arian until the death of Valens in 378. The occupants of many ecclesiastical sees changed with every passing emperor, episcopal elections were contested, allies were necessary. With respect to the Christmas rhetoric, Susan Roll suggests that putting the feast to such a use represented "control issues"—"emphasizing certain themes to influence members of the church away from particular practices, teachings, ideas and sympathies, and toward others more congenial to the interests of church leadership."[6] She goes on to say, "The fact that this occurs in the context not of theological debate but of rite, prayer and celebration which takes place in a more subjectively open, less critical context, represents an insidious form of control."[7] In fact, our preachers *did* engage in polemics in other forums, but such treatises and correspondence would not have been very accessible to the average church member. As noted before, the pulpit and the martyrium were the important points of contact between bishop and faithful.

It is also interesting that although the surviving correspondence among our group of preachers yields some information about saints' days, activities at martyrs' tombs and the practice of giving gifts at holidays, it does not contain their thoughts about what we consider the *big* liturgical developments of the period, such as the adoption of Christmas and the appearance of the Feast of the Ascension. One would think that if these developments were as sudden and conscious as has been suggested, there would be some discussion in the letters around how that strategy was working out. Instead the epistolary evidence contains the business of dealing with personal and professional issues of all kinds, particularly those of ecclesiastical politics in a state whose emperor could be Arian one year and Nicene the next.

As is true today, fourth-century feasts drew larger than normal crowds to churches and martyrs' tombs. Homilies on those occasions can be important opportunities for reaching a larger audience with the crucial points of a preacher's theological agenda. The Cappadocian and Pontic homilies we have gathered together and examined through the lens of doctrinal controversy are rich sites for exploring what our preachers thought was important and how they used their homiletical opportunities to refute opposing theology, to teach their own theology and to promote internal ecclesial cohesion. As we have seen, these homilies also yield important information about the developing liturgical calendars of this corner of the eastern Roman Empire in late antiquity.

However, there is still work to be done on this material. Studying the homilies gathered in this book within other methodological frameworks would undoubtedly yield further insights and would perhaps shed light on some points that remain unclear. In addition, closer study of the material for specific clues about psalmody and scripture readings may answer still other questions about liturgical year practice in these areas. For example, if one could identify whether the Cappadocians favored a particular gospel, this might lead to further clarity about why they celebrated particular feasts and not others. Finally, additional comparative work with, say, the homilies of John Chrysostom or the sources from Jerusalem would help to flesh out the area of the liturgical year map begun in these pages.

Notes

1.   Delehaye, *Origines*, 91.

2.   Bernardi points out that although Basil mentions that he is preaching at the martyrium of the forty, it is probably in Caesarea, not Sebaste, since relics of these martyrs were translated to many places, including the West (Bernardi, 83).

3.   Augustine of Hippo, Sermon 202.2, *The Works of Saint Augustine: A Translation for the 21st Century*, part 3: *Sermons*, vol. 6: *Sermons 184–229Z*, trans. Edmund Hill, ed. John Rotelle (New Rochelle, New York: New City Press, 1992), pp. 91–92.

4.   Asterius of Amaseia, "On the Festival of the Calends" 2, *Ancient Sermons*, 114–115.

5.   Ibid. 3, *Ancient Sermons*, 115–116.

6.   Roll, 166.

7.   Ibid.

Works Consulted

Cappadocian Primary Sources

Amphilochius of Iconium. *De recens baptizatis*. E. Dekkers, *et al*, gen. eds. *Corpus Christianorum*, Series Graeca. Vol. 3, *Amphilochii Iconiensis Opera*. Edited by Cornelis Datema. Brepols: Leuven University Press, 1978.

————. *In diem Sabbati Sancti*. E. Dekkers, *et al*, gen. eds. *Corpus Christianorum*, Series Graeca. Vol. 3, *Amphilochii Iconiensis Opera*. Edited by Cornelis Datema. Brepols: Leuven University Press, 1978.

————. *In mesopentecosten* (spurious). E. Dekkers, *et al*, gen. eds. *Corpus Christianorum*, Series Graeca. Vol. 3, *Amphilochii Iconiensis Opera*. Edited by Cornelis Datema. Brepols: Leuven University Press, 1978.

————. *In natalitia Domini*. E. Dekkers, *et al*, gen. eds. *Corpus Christianorum*, Series Graeca. Vol. 3, *Amphilochii Iconiensis Opera*. Edited by Cornelis Datema. Brepols: Leuven University Press, 1978.

Asterius of Amasea. *Against Covetousness*. *Sermons for Modern Times by Asterius,Bishop of Amasia* [*sic*] *Circa 375–405 A.D.* Translated by Galusha Anderson and Edgar Johnson Goodspeed. New York: The Pilgrim Press, 1904

————. *Enarratio in martyrium praeclarissimae martyris Euphemiae*. *Asterius of Amasea Homilies I–XIV: Text, Introduction and Notes*. Edited by C. Datema. Leiden: E.J. Brill, 1970.

————. *Encomium in sanctos martyres*. *Asterius of Amasea Homilies I–XIV: Text, Introduction and Notes*. Edited by C. Datema. Leiden: E.J. Brill, 1970.

————. *In S. Martyrem Phocam*. *Asterius of Amasea Homilies I–XIV: Text,Introduction and Notes*. Edited by C. Datema. Leiden: E.J. Brill, 1970.

————. *Laudatio S. protomartyris Stephani*. *Asterius of Amasea Homilies I–XIV: Text, Introduction and Notes*. Edited by C. Datema. Leiden: E.J. Brill, 1970.

————. *On the Festival of the Calends*. *Sermons for Modern Times by Asterius, Bishop of Amasia* [*sic*] *Circa 375–405 A.D.* Translated by Galusha Anderson and Edgar Johnson Goodspeed. New York: The Pilgrim Press, 1904

————. *Oratio in principium jejuniorum*. *Asterius of Amasea Homilies I-XIV: Text, Introduction and Notes*. Edited by C. Datema. Leiden: E.J. Brill, 1970.

Basil of Caesarea. *De gratiarum actione*. *Patrologiae Cursus Completus*, Series Graeca. Edited by J.-P. Migne. Vol. 31. [Paris: n.p.], 1857.

————. *De jejunio* I. *Patrologiae Cursus Completus*, Series Graeca. Edited by J.-P. Migne. Vol. 31. [Paris: n.p.], 1857.

————. *De jejunio* II. *Patrologiae Cursus Completus*, Series Graeca. Edited by J.-P. Migne. Vol. 31. [Paris: n.p.], 1857.

————. *Exhortatoria ad baptisma sanctum*. *Patrologiae Cursus Completus*, Series Graeca. Edited by J.-P. Migne. Vol. 31. [Paris: n.p.], 1857.

————. *In ebriosos*. *Patrologiae Cursus Completus*, Series Graeca. Edited by J.-P. Migne. Vol. 31. [Paris: n.p.], 1857.

————. *In Gordium martyrem*. *Patrologiae Cursus Completus*, Series Graeca. Edited by J.-P. Migne. Vol. 31. [Paris: n.p.], 1857.

——. *In martyrem Julittam. Patrologiae Cursus Completus*, Series Graeca. Edited by J.-P. Migne. Vol. 31. [Paris: n.p.], 1857.

——. *In sanctam Christi generationem. Opera omnia quae exstant vel quae ejus nomine circumferuntur*. Edited by Julian Garnier. Vol. 2, pt. 1. Paris: Gaume Fratres, 1839.

——. *In sanctum martyrem Mamantem. Patrologiae Cursus Completus*, Series Graeca. Edited by J.-P. Migne. Vol. 31. [Paris: n.p.], 1857.

——. *In sanctos quadraginta martyres. Patrologiae Cursus Completus*, Series Graeca. Edited by J.-P. Migne. Vol. 31. [Paris: n.p.], 1857.

——. *On the Holy Spirit. Nicene and Post-Nicene Fathers*. A Select Library of the Christian Church, Second Series. Edited by Philip Schaff and Henry Wace. Vol. 8, *St. Basil: Letters and Select Works*. Grand Rapids, Mich.: Wm. B. Eerdmans Publishing Co., 1899.

——. *The Hexaemeron. Nicene and Post-Nicene Fathers*. A Select Library of the Christian Church, Second Series. Edited by Philip Schaff and Henry Wace. Vol. 8, *St. Basil: Letters and Select Works*. Grand Rapids, Mich.: Wm. B. Eerdmans Publishing Co., 1899.

——. *Epistles* 49, 58, 93, 100, 120, 142, 155, 164, 176, 188, 197, 199, 200–202, 217, 232–236, 252. *The Fathers of the Church: A New Translation*. St. Basil's Letters, 2 vols. Translated by Agnes Clare Way. Edited by Roy J. Deferrari. New York: Fathers of the Church, Inc., 1955.

Gregory of Nazianzus. *Concerning His Own Life. The Fathers of the Church: A New Translation*. Vol. 75, *Saint Gregory of Nazianzus: Three Poems*. Translated by Denis Molaise Meehan. Washington, D.C.: The Catholic University of America Press, 1987.

——. *Epistles* 1, 9, 25–28, 63, 72–74, 76, 122, 171, 182, 184, 197. *Nicene and Post-Nicene Fathers*. A Select Library of the Christian Church, Second Series. Edited by Philip Schaff and Henry Wace. Vol. 7, *S. Cyril of Jerusalem. S. Gregory Nazianzen*. Grand Rapids, Mich.: Wm. B. Eerdmans Publishing Co., 1899.

——. *Oration 1 On Easter and His Reluctance. Nicene and Post-Nicene Fathers*. A Select Library of the Christian Church, Second Series. Edited by Philip Schaff and Henry Wace. Vol. 7, *S. Cyril of Jerusalem. S. Gregory Nazianzen*. Grand Rapids, Mich.: Wm. B. Eerdmans Publishing Co., 1899.

——. *Oration 38 On the Theophany, or Birthday of Christ. Nicene and Post-Nicene Fathers*. A Select Library of the Christian Church, Second Series. Edited by Philip Schaff and Henry Wace. Vol. 7, *S. Cyril of Jerusalem. S. Gregory Nazianzen*. Grand Rapids, Mich.: Wm. B. Eerdmans Publishing Co., 1899.

——. *Oration 39 Oration on the Holy Lights. Nicene and Post-Nicene Fathers*. A Select Library of the Christian Church, Second Series. Edited by Philip Schaff and Henry Wace. Vol. 7, *S. Cyril of Jerusalem. S. Gregory Nazianzen*. Grand Rapids, Mich.: Wm. B. Eerdmans Publishing Co., 1899.

——. *Oration 40 The Oration on Holy Baptism. Nicene and Post-Nicene Fathers*. A Select Library of the Christian Church, Second Series. Edited by Philip Schaff and Henry Wace. Vol. 7, *S. Cyril of Jerusalem. S. Gregory Nazianzen*. Grand Rapids, Mich.: Wm. B. Eerdmans Publishing Co., 1899.

——. *Oration 41 On Pentecost. Nicene and Post-Nicene Fathers*. A Select Library of the Christian Church, Second Series. Edited by Philip Schaff and Henry Wace. Vol. 7, *S. Cyril of Jerusalem. S. Gregory Nazianzen*. Grand Rapids, Mich.: Wm. B. Eerdmans Publishing Co., 1899.

————. *Oration 43 The Panegyric on S. Basil. Nicene and Post-Nicene Fathers*. A Select Library of the Christian Church, Second Series. Edited by Philip Schaff and Henry Wace. Vol. 7, *S. Cyril of Jerusalem. S. Gregory Nazianzen*. Grand Rapids, Mich.: Wm. B. Eerdmans Publishing Co., 1899.

————. *Oration 44 In Novam Dominicam. Patrologiae Cursus Completus*, Series Graeca. Edited by J.-P. Migne. Vol. 36. Paris: Migne, 1858.

————. *Oration 45 The Second Oration on Easter. Nicene and Post-Nicene Fathers*. A Select Library of the Christian Church, Second Series. Edited by Philip Schaff and Henry Wace. Vol. 7, *S. Cyril of Jerusalem. S. Gregory Nazianzen*. Grand Rapids, Mich.: Wm. B. Eerdmans Publishing Co., 1899.

Gregory of Nyssa. *Epistles* 1, 11, 13–16, 18, 121. *Nicene and Post-Nicene Fathers*. A Select Library of the Christian Church, Second Series. Edited by Philip Schaff and Henry Wace. Vol. 5, *Gregory of Nyssa: Dogmatic Treatises, Etc*. Grand Rapids, Mich.: Wm. B. Eerdmans Publishing Co., 1954.

————. *Discourse on the Holy Pascha. The Easter Sermons of Gregory of Nyssa: Translation and Commentary*. Translated by S. G. Hall. Edited by Andreas Spira and Christoph Klock. Cambridge: Mass., 1981.

————. *Eulogy for Basil the Great. The Gregory of Nyssa Homepage*. Translated by Richard (Casimir)McCambly.
http://www.bhsu.edu/artssciences/asfaculty/dsalomon/nyssa/home.html

————. *In ascensionem Christi. Gregorii Nysseni Opera*. Edited by W. Jaeger, *et al.* Vol. 9, *Sermones Pars I*. Edited by Gunterus Heil, *et al.* Leiden: E.J. Brill, 1967.

————. *In diem natalem salvatoris. Gregorii Nysseni Opera*. Edited by W. Jaeger, *et al.* Vol. 10.2, *Sermones Pars III*. Edited by Ernestus Rhein, *et al.* Leiden: E.J. Brill, 1996.

————. *In luciferam sanctam Domini resurrectionem. Gregorii Nysseni Opera*. Edited by W. Jaeger, *et al.* Vol. 9, *Sermones Pars I*. Edited by Gunterus Heil, *et al.* Leiden: E.J. Brill, 1967.

————. *In Praise of Blessed Theodore, The Great Martyr. The Gregory of Nyssa Homepage*. Translated by Richard (Casimir) McCambly.
www.bhsu.edu/artssciences/asfaculty/dsalomon/nyssa/. *Gregorii Nysseni Opera*. Edited by W. Jaeger, *et al.* Vol. 10.1, *Sermones Pars II*. Edited by Gunterus Heil, *et al.* Leiden: E.J. Brill, 1990.

————. *In sanctam Pentecosten. Gregorii Nysseni Opera*. Edited by W. Jaeger, *et al.* Vol. 10.2, *Sermones Pars III*. Edited by Ernestus Rhein, *et al.* Leiden: E.J. Brill, 1996.

————. *On the Baptism of Christ. Nicene and Post-Nicene Fathers*. A Select Library of the Christian Church, Second Series. Edited by Philip Schaff and Henry Wace. Vol. 5, *Gregory of Nyssa: Dogmatic Treatises, Etc*. Grand Rapids, Mich.: Wm. B. Eerdmans Publishing Co., 1954.

————. *On the Making of Man. Nicene and Post-Nicene Fathers*. A Select Library of the Christian Church, Second Series. Edited by Philip Schaff and Henry Wace. Vol. 5, *Gregory of Nyssa: Dogmatic Treatises, Etc*. Grand Rapids, Mich.: Wm. B. Eerdmans Publishing Co., 1954.

————. *On the Three-Day Period of the Resurrection of our Lord Jesus Christ. The Easter Sermons of Gregory of Nyssa:Translation and Commentary*. Translated by S. G. Hall. Edited by Andreas Spira and Christoph Klock. Cambridge: Mass., 1981.

————. *The Holy and Saving Pascha. The Easter Sermons of Gregory of Nyssa: Translation and Commentary*. Translated by S. G. Hall. Edited by Andreas Spira and Christoph Klock. Cambridge: Mass., 1981.

————. *The Life of Gregory the Wonderworker. The Fathers of the Church: A New Translation.* Edited by Thomas P. Halton *et al.* Vol. 98, *St. Gregory Thaumaturgus Life and Works.* Translated by Michael Slusser. Washington, D.C.: The Catholic University Press, 1998.

————. *Two Homilies Concerning Stephen, Protomartyr. The Gregory of Nyssa Homepage.* Translated   by   Richard   (Casimir)   McCambly. http://www.bhsu.edu/artssciences/asfaculty/dsalomon/nyssa/home.html.   *Gregorii Nysseni Opera.* Edited by W. Jaeger, *et al.* Vol. 10.1, *Sermones Pars II.* Edited by Gunterus Heil, *et al.* Leiden: E.J. Brill, 1990.

————. *Two Homilies Concerning the Forty Martyrs. The Gregory of Nyssa Homepage.* Translated   by   Richard   (Casimir)   McCambly. http://www.bhsu.edu/artssciences/asfaculty/dsalomon/nyssa/home.html.   *Gregorii Nysseni Opera.* Edited by W. Jaeger, *et al.* Vol. 10.1, *Sermones Pars II.* Edited by Gunterus Heil, *et al.* Leiden: E.J. Brill, 1990.

Other Primary Sources

Athanasius of Alexandria. Festal Letters. *Nicene and Post-Nicene Fathers. A Select Library of the Christian Church,* Second Series. Edited by Philip Schaff and Henry Wace. Vol. 4, *Athanasius: Select Writings and Letters.* Grand Rapids, Mich.: Wm. B. Eerdmans Publishing Co., 1899.

Augustine, Sermon 198 On 1 January, Against the Pagans. *The Works of Saint Augustine: Translation for the 21ˢᵗ Century.* Vol. 3, Sermons, part 6, *On the Liturgical Seasons.* Translated by Edmund Hill. Edited by E. Rotelle. New Rochelle, NY: New City Press, 1993.

Egeria. *Egeria's Travels.* Translated by John Wilkinson. London: SPCK, 1971.

Epiphanius of Salamis. *The Panarion of Epiphanius of Salamis: Books II and III.* Translated by Frank Williams. Nag Hammadi and Manichaean Studies 36. Edited by J.M. Robinson and H.J. Klimkeit. Leiden: E.J. Brill, 1994.

Eusebius of Caesarea. *Ecclesiastical History.* 2 vols. Translated by Roy J. Deferrari. The Fathers of the Church 19. Edited by Roy J. Deferrari et al. New York: Fathers of the Church, Inc., 1953.

Firmilian of Caesarea. Letter to Cyprian. *The Ante-Nicene Fathers.* Edited by Alexander Roberts and James Donaldson. Vol. 5, *Hippolytus, Cyprian, Caius, Novatian, Appendix.* New York: Charles Scribner's Sons, 1926.

Le Typikon de la Grande Église. Edited and translated by Juan Mateos. Vol. 1, Le Cycle des Douze Mois. Vol. 2, Le Cycle des Fêtes Mobiles. Orientalia Christiana Analecta 166. Rome: Pont. Institutum Orientalium Studiorum, 1962–1963.

Martyriologium Hieronymianum. Edited by I.B. De Rossi and L. Duchesne. N.P., n.d.

Socrates Scholasticus. *The Ecclesiastical History. Nicene and Post-Nicene Fathers. A Select Library of the Christian Church,* Second Series. Edited by Philip Schaff and Henry Wace. Vol. 2, *Socrates, Sozomenus: Church Histories.* Grand Rapids, Mich.: Wm. B. Eerdmans Publishing Co., 1899.

Sozomen. *The Ecclesiastical History. Nicene and Post-Nicene Fathers. A Select Library of the Christian Church,* Second Series. Edited by Philip Schaff and Henry Wace. Vol. 2, *Socrates, Sozomenus: Church Histories.* Grand Rapids, Mich.: Wm. B. Eerdmans Publishing Co., 1899.

Secondary Sources

Adam, Adolf. *The Liturgical Year*. New York: Pueblo, 1981.

Alexander, J. Neil. *Waiting for the Coming: The Liturgical Meaning of Advent, Christmas, Epiphany*. Washington, D.C.: The Pastoral Press, 1993.

————. "Principal Aspects of Sacred Time in Byzantine Jerusalem." Th.D. diss., The General Theological Seminary, 1993.

Auf der Maur, Hansjörg. *Die Osterhomilien der Asterios Sophistes als Quelle für die Geschichte der Osterfeier*. Trierer theologische studien 17. Trier: Paulinus-Verlag, 1967.

Bainton, Roland H. "The Origins of Epiphany." In *Early and Medieval Christianity: The Collected Papers in Church History*. Series One. Boston: Beacon Press, 1962.

Baldovin, John F. *The Urban Character of Christian Worship: The Origins, Development, and Meaning of Stational Liturgy*. Orientalia Christiana Analecta, ed. Robert F. Taft, no. 228. Rome: Pont. Institutum Studiorum Orientalium, 1987.

Baumstark, Anton. *Comparative Liturgy*. Westminster, MD: Newman, 1958.

Beckwith, Roger T. "The Origins of the Festivals of Easter and Whitsun." *Studia Liturgica* 13 (1979): 1–20.

Bernardi, Jean. *La prédication des Pères Cappadociens*. Paris: Presses Universitaires de France, 1968.

Botte, Bernard. *Les origines de la Noël et de l'Épiphanie*. Textes et études liturgiques 1. Louvain: Abbaye du Mont César, 1932.

Bradshaw, Paul F. *The Search for the Origins of Christian Worship: Sources and Methods for the Study of Early Liturgy*. New York: Oxford University Press, 1992.

————. "The Origins of Easter." In *Passover and Easter: Origin and History to Modern Times. Two Liturgical Traditions*, ed. Paul F. Bradshaw and Lawrence A. Hoffman, no. 5. Notre Dame, Ind.: University of Notre Dame Press, 1999.

Brown, Peter. *The Cult of the Saints: Its Rise and Function in Latin Christianity*. The Haskell Lectures on History of Religions, ed. Joseph M. Kitagawa, New Series no. 2. Chicago: The University of Chicago Press, 1981.

Burnett, Jill S. "Looking Forward to Epiphany," *Liturgy* 14.2 (Summer 1997): 9–17.

Cabié, Robert. *La Pentecôte: l'évolution de la cinquantaine pascale au cours des cinq premiers siècles*. Edited by A.-G. Martimort. Bibliothèque de Liturgie. Tournai: Desclée & Co., 1965.

Cantalamessa, Raniero. *Easter in the Early Church: An Anthology of Jewish and Early Christian Texts*, rev. ed. Translated by James M. Quigley and Joseph T. Lienhard Collegeville, Minn.: The Liturgical Press, 1993.

Carroll, Thomas K. and Thomas Halton. *Liturgical Practice in the Fathers. Message of the Fathers*, ed. Thomas Halton, no. 21. Wilmington, Del.: Michael Glazier, 1988.

Chupungco, Anscar J. *Shaping the Easter Feast*. NPM Studies in Church Music and Liturgy. Washington: D.C., 1992.

Connell, Martin. "The Liturgical Year in Northern Italy (365–450)." Ph.D. diss., University of Notre Dame, 1994.

Courtonne, Yves. *Un Témoin du IVe Siècle Oriental: Saint Basile et son Temps d'après sa Correspondance. Collection d'Études Anciennes*. Paris: Sociéte d'Édition «Les Belles Lettres,» 1973.

Cullmann, Oscar. *Noël dans l'Église ancienne*. Cahiers Théologiques de l'Actualité Protestante, ed. J.-J. von Allmen et al, no. 25. Neuchâtel: Delachaux & Niestlé, 1949.

Daniélou, Jean. "La chronologie des sermons de Grégoire de Nysse." *Revue des sciences religieuses* 29 (1955): 346–72.

―――. "Les origines de l'épiphanie et les testimonia." In *Noël, Épiphanie, Retour du Christ,* Lex Orandi, ed. A.M. Dubarle et al, no. 40. Paris: Éditions due Cerf, 1967.

―――. "Grégoire de Nysse et l'origine de la fête de l'Ascension." In *Kyriakon: Festschrift Johannes Quasten,* edited by Patrick Granfield and Josef A. Jungmann, 663–66. Münster: Aschendorff, 1970.

Delehaye, Hippolyte. *Légendes hagiographiques,* 3d ed. Subsidia Hagiographica, no. 18. Brussels: Société des Bollandistes, 1927.

―――. *Les Origines du Culte des Martyrs,* 2d rev. ed. Subsidia Hagiographica, no. 20. Brussels: Société des Bollandistes, 1933.

Denis-Boulet, Noële M. *The Christian Calendar.* Translated by P. Hepburne-Scott. New York: Hawthorn Books, 1960.

Dix, Gregory. *The Shape of the Liturgy,* 2d. ed. Westminster, England: Dacre Press, 1945; reprint 1954.

Fedwick, Paul Jonathan. *The Church and the Charisma of Leadership in Basil of Caesarea.* Studies and Texts, no. 45. Toronto: Pontifical Institute of Mediaeval Studies, 1979.

―――. "A Chronology of the Life and Works of Basil of Caesarea." In *Basil of Caesarea: Christian, Humanist, Ascetic: A Sixteen-Hundredth Anniversary Symposium.* Part One. Edited by Paul Jonathan Fedwick. Toronto: Pontifical Institute of Mediaeval Studies, 1981.

Forlin Patrucco, Marcella. "Social Patronage and Political Mediation in the Activity of Basil of Caesarea." In *Studia Patristica* 17.3, 1102–1107. Elmsford, NY: Pergamon Press, 1982.

Gain, Benoît. *L'église de Cappadoce au IVᵉ siècle d'après la correspondance de Basile de Césarée (330–379).* OCA, no. 225. Rome: Pontificium Institutum Orientale, 1985.

Gribomont, Jean. "Notes biographiques sur s. Basile le Grand." In *Basil of Caesarea: Christian, Humanist, Ascetic: A Sixteen-Hundredth Anniversary Symposium.* Part One. Edited by Paul Jonathan Fedwick. Toronto: Pontifical Institute of Mediaeval Studies, 1981.

Gunstone, John. *The Feast of Pentecost: The Great Fifty Days in the Liturgy.* London: The Faith Press, 1967.

―――. *Christmas and Epiphany.* London: The Faith Press, 1967.

Holman, Susan R. *The Hungry are Dying: Beggars and Bishops in Roman Cappadocia.* Oxford Studes in Historical Theology, ed. David C. Steinmetz. Oxford: Oxford University Press, 2001.

Huber, Wolfgang. *Passa und Ostern: Untersuchungen zur Osterfeier der alten Kirche.* Berlin: Verlag Alfred Töpelmann, 1969.

Johnson, Maxwell, E. "Preparation for Pascha? Lent in Christian Antiquity." In *Between Memory and Hope: Readings on the Liturgical Year.* Edited by Maxwell E. Johnson. Collegeville, Minn.: The Liturgical Press, 2000.

Jones, A.H.M. *The Cities of the Eastern Roman Provinces,* 2d ed. Oxford: The Clarendon Press, 1971.

Kelly, J.N.D. *Early Christian Doctrines,* rev. ed. San Francisco: HarperSanFrancisco, 1978.

Kinzig, Wolfram. *In Search of Asterius: Studies on the Authorship of the Homilies on the Psalms.* Forschungen zur Kirchen- und Dogmengeschichte, no. 47. Göttingen, Germany: Vandenhoeck & Ruprecht, 1990.

Kopecek, Thomas A. "Cappadocian Fathers and Civic Patriotism." *Church History* 43 (1974): 293–303.

Kretschmar, Georg. "Himmelfahrt und Pfingsten." *Zeitschrift für Kirchengeschichte* Folge IV, no. Band 66.3 (1954–1955): 209–53.

Loofs, Friedrich. *Eustathius von Sebaste und die Chronologie der Basilius-Briefe: Eine patristische Studie*. Halle, Germany: Niemeyer, 1898.

Matthews, John. *The Roman Empire of Ammianus*. Baltimore: The Johns Hopkins University Press, 1989.

McArthur, A. Allan. *The Evolution of the Christian Year*. Greenwich, Conn.: The Seabury Press, 1953.

McGuckin, John. *Saint Gregory of Nazianzus: An Intellectual Biography*. Crestwood, NY: St. Vladimir's Seminary Press, 2001.

Meredith, S.J., Anthony. "The Answer to Jewish Objections (De Tridui Spatio 294,14– 298,18). In *The Easter Sermons of Gregory of Nyssa: Translation and Commentary*. Patristic Monograph Series, ed. Andreas Spira and Christoph Klock, no. 9. Cambridge, Mass.: The Philadelphia Patristic Foundation, 1981.

———. *The Cappadocians*. Crestwood, NY: St. Vladimir's Seminary Press, 1995.

———. *Gregory of Nyssa*. London: Routledge, 1999.

Mossay, Justin. *Les fêtes de noël et de l'épiphanie d'après les sources cappadociennes du IVè siècle*. Louvain: Abbaye du Mont César, 1965.

Moutsoulas, Elie D. "Les sermons pascaux de Grégoire de Nysse." *Theologia* 51 (1980): 333– 47.

Nocent, Adrian. *The Liturgical Year*. Collegeville, MN: The Liturgical Press, 1977.

Otis, Brooks. "Gregory of Nyssa and the Cappadocian Conception of Time." In *Studia Patristica* 14, ed. Elizabeth A. Livingstone, 327–357. Berlin: Akademie-Verlag, 1976.

Regan, Patrick. "The Fifty Days and the Fiftieth Day." *Worship* 55 (1981): 194–218.

Roll, Susan K. *Toward the Origins of Christmas*. Kampen, The Netherlands: Kok Pharos Publishing House, 1995.

Rousseau, Philip. *Basil of Caesarea*. Transformation of the Classical Heritage, no. 20. Berkeley: University of California Press, 1994.

Ruether, Rosemary Radford. *Gregory of Nazianzus: Rhetor and Philosopher*. Oxford: The Clarendon Press, 1969.

Salaville, Sévérien. "Τεσσαρακοστή, Ascension et Pentecôte au IVᵉ siècle." *Echos d'Orient* 28 (1929): 257–71.

Samuel, Alan E. *Greek and Roman Chronology: Calendars and Years in Classical Antiquity*. Munich: C.H. Beck'sche Verlagsbuchhandlung, 1972.

Stewart-Sykes, Alistair. *The Lamb's High Feast: Melito, Peri Pascha and the Quartodeciman Paschal Liturgy at Sardis*. Supplements to Vigiliae Christianae, ed. J. Den Boeft et al, no. 42. Leiden: Brill, 1998.

Taft, Robert. "The Structural Analysis of Liturgical Units: An Essay in Methodology." In *Beyond East & West: Problems in Liturgical Understanding*. NPM Studies in Church Music and Liturgy. Washington, DC.: The Pastoral Press, 1984.

———. "Historicism Revisited." In *Beyond East and West: Problems in Liturgical Understanding*, 15–30. Washington, D.C.: The Pastoral Press, 1984.

———. "Comparative Liturgy Fifty Years After Anton Baumstark (d. 1948): A Reply to Recent Critics." *Worship* 73 (1999): 521–540.

Talley, Thomas J. *The Origins of the Liturgical Year*, 2d. ed. Collegeville, MN: The Liturgical Press, 1991.

———. "Constantine and Christmas." In *Between Memory and Hope: Readings on the Liturgical Year*. Edited by Maxwell E. Johnson. Collegeville, Minn.: The Liturgical Press, 2000.

Theodorou, Evangelos. "Saint Jean Chrysostome et la Fête de Noël." In *Noël-Épiphanie Retour du Christ*. Lex Orandi, ed. A.-M. Dubarle et al, no. 40. Paris: Les Éditions du Cerf, 1967.

Usener, Hermann. *Das Weihnachtsfest*, 3d. ed. Bonn: H. Bouvier u. Co. Verlag, 1969.

Van Dam, Raymond. "Emperor, Bishops and Friends in Late Antique Cappadocia." *Journal of Theological Studies* n.s. 37:1 (1986): 442–447.

Van Goudoever, J. *Biblical Calendars*. Leiden: E. J. Brill, 1961.

Wilken, Robert L. "Liturgy, Bible and Theology in the Easter Homilies of Gregory of Nyssa." In *Écriture et Culture Philosophique dans la Pensée de Grégoire de Nysse: Actes du Colloque de Chevetogne* (22–26 Septembre 1969), edited by Marguerite Harl, 127–43. Leiden: E.J. Brill, 1971.

West, Fritz. *The Comparative Liturgy of Anton Baumstark*. Alcuin/GROW Liturgical Study, no. 31. Bramcote, Nottingham: Grove Books, 1995.

Winslow, Donald F. *The Dynamics of Salvation: A Study in Gregory of Nazianzus*. Patristic Monograph Series, no. 7. Cambridge, MA: Philadelphia Patristic Foundation, 1979.

Index

PATRISTIC STUDIES
Gerald Bray, *General Editor*

This is a series of monographs designed to provide access to research at the cutting-edge of current Patristic Studies. Particular attention will be given to the development of Christian theology during the first five centuries of the Church and to the different types of Biblical interpretation which the Fathers used. Each study will engage with modern discussion of the theme being treated, but will also break new ground in original textual research. In exceptional cases, a volume may consist of the critical edition of a text, with notes and references, as well as translation. Revised doctoral dissertations may also be published, though the main focus of the series will be on more mature research and reflection. Each volume will be about 250–300 pages (100,000–120,000 words) long, with a full bibliography and index.

Inquiries and manuscripts should be directed to:

Acquisitions Department
Peter Lang Publishing, Inc.
P.O. Box 1246
Bel Air, MD 21014-1246

To order other books in this series, please contact our Customer Service Department at:

(800) 770-LANG (within the U.S.)
(212) 647-7706 (outside the U.S.)
(212) 647-7707 FAX

or browse online by series at:

www.peterlangusa.com